1918 Ford Model "T"

1919 Franklin

1920 Chevrolet

1924 Chandler

1925 Locomobile

1926 Kissel

1930 Cord L-29

1931 Durant

1932 Essex

1936 Terraplane

1937 LaSalle

1938 Ford

1942 Lincoln Continental

1945 Ford Staff Car

1946 DeSoto

1950 Pontiac

1951 Nash

1952 Plymouth

1956 Dodge

1957 Ford Thunderbird

1958 DeSoto

1962 Ford Falcon

1963 Dodge

1964 Chevrolet Impala

THE PICTORIAL TREASURY OF
CLASSIC AMERICAN AUTOMOBILES

THE PICTORIAL TREASURY OF
CLASSIC
AMERICAN
AUTOMOBILES

Timothy Jacobs & Tom Debolski

GALLERY BOOKS
An imprint of W.H. Smith Publishers Inc.
112 Madison Avenue
New York, New York 10016

Published by Gallery Books
A Division of W H Smith Publishers Inc
112 Madison Avenue
New York, New York 10016

Produced by
Brompton Books Corp
15 Sherwood Place
Greenwich, CT 06830

ISBN 0-8317-6906-8

Printed in Hong Kong

10 9 8 7 6 5 4 3 2 1

Page 1: The Duesenberg SJ Roadster pictured here represents what many believe to be the very apex of American automotive styling. This legendary car was renowned for its speed as well as its brash but elegant styling. A combination of visionary genius and technical expertise came together in this beautiful car that could attain 130 mph.

Pages 2–3: Another representative of the best is this 1931 Packard phaeton. Since the 1920s, Packard shared the spotlight at the top level of American luxury with few other cars, and its distinctively large radiator was a hallmark of mechanical perfection and luxuriant comfort the world over. Packard, a legend in its own time, served to inspire the very best in automobiles of our present age.

These pages: An elegant 1955 Ford Thunderbird convertible. It was one of the fastest cars in America when it came out, and the Thunderbird's two-seat coziness combined with power and appointments usually found in much larger cars to make it an instant sensation, and an enduring symbol of all that is uniquely American.

INTRODUCTION 6

AT THE HEAD OF THE LINE 8

THE AMERICAN AUTO
COMES OF AGE 24

LUXURY MEETS THE
STREAMLINED FAMILY CAR 38

THE UNFORGETTABLE 1950s 96

SIMPLE LINES AND
BIG HORSEPOWER 166

INTRODUCTION

The internal-combustion automobile has been with us for over 100 years, and in that time, it has both undergone an astonishing amount of change, and has paradoxically stayed the same, with its stylistic variants going in and out of vogue over and over again, in a virtual merry-go-round of appearances. Outside of this genre, there were such great cars as the Stanley Steamer and the classic electric cars that had to be recharged every evening, all of which types were soon buried under the cultural obsession with the versatile and reliable gasoline engine.

There is hardly a person in the United States who does not in some way depend upon the automobile for a daily mode of transportation, and there are more cars involved in the average American interurban traffic jam than even exist in many other entire *countries* in the Western world. Perhaps that is why American cars are so indentifiably American; there are so many that sheer abundance is an outstanding characteristic, and the sheer quantity of makes and models produces a specific stylistic gravity of its own, making possible a sense of 'the classic American car.'

Our definition here of 'classic' American automobiles includes those that are definitely *of* an era, either by dint of complete conformity with that era's styling modes, or by complete departure from them — or by dint of the fact that when you look at a particular car, a particular milieu is immediately evoked. What makes a car 'great' is the rich net of associations that surrounds it, whether it is the tiny Austin American roadster of the 1930s or the sleek Cadillac Eldorado of the late 1950s. This book has no pretense of being comprehensive: it is a visit to a gallery of personal selections. Also, steam and electric-driven cars are not included here, due to their existence outside the mainstream of internal combustion-engined models.

Back in the 1890s and early 1900s, newspapers carried lurid accounts of 'motorcar' drivers roaring through rural hamlets, terrorizing people and traumatizing livestock. Early manufacturers even provided cars with exhaust cutouts that temporarily increased their power and noise. Still, it took a very short time for the general populace to accept the automobile as an enduring replacement for the horse, and it was not long after that the new machines became a major American symbol of power and prestige.

Safety features such as horns and improved brakes had combined with a popular curiosity (about what life was like at 30 miles per hour) to make the 'motorcar' an object of increasingly broader desirability. This acceptance grew by leaps and bounds, and soon the motoring public clamored for yet newer shapes and sizes, the latest in body detailing, the latest in powerplants, and the type of styling that would clearly reflect the private owner's values and sense of self-worth.

The luxury car builders of the 1920s and 1930s went further than the average motorist usually dreamed. They built such paragons of all-out performance and luxury as the Packard, the Duesenberg and the Pierce-Arrow, which not only trounced the racing competition and set records, but also looked, rode and handled as well as they performed. The average motorist usually settled for his own version of the Packard V-12 or the supercharged Duesenberg — the Ford V-8 coupe or the Pontiac roadster, which (with lots of help from the driver's imagination) imitated the panther-like swiftness and the sporty styling of the more expensive cars.

Be that as it may, the Ford, the Chevrolet, the Chrysler and other low-to-medium priced cars created their own definition of the motoring scene — and they pushed on through the turbulent 1930s to new frontiers, while many of the grander makes were forced, by the unstable financial climate, to halt production.

At times, American auto styling has taken rather unusual forms — as is witnessed to by the first Chrysler Airflow cars of the late 1930s, resplendent in all their pug-nosed strangeness. At times, too, the American milieu produced cars of exquisite beauty and style — Auburn, Cord and Duesenberg; the Packards of the 'glory years' and the Lincoln Continentals of the

1930s and 1940s are a few of the dazzling examples that come to mind.

Perhaps no decade displayed as unique a sense of styling as the 1950s, with its brash, bold use of chrome, wraparound windshields and sweeping, jet-aircraft inspired tailfins. In the 1960s, the car buyer could purchase a factory-built highway missile that would do well at any drag race! And so it is, in the American automotive parade; all this and more is contained in the annals of the great American classic cars.

Of the various 'ages' of American automotive engineering, the 1950s had the most truly extroverted character. Large chrome grilles, flashy styling and boldly stated two-tone paint jobs made motoring a matter of catching the attention of passers-by with the latest in Detroit excess. Not all of it was bad, much of it was very interesting, and the continuing incursion of jet aircraft motifs made automobile styling in the 1950s era rather exciting. Shown *below* is one of the better designed 1950s cars, a 1956 Oldsmobile Starfire convertible, complete with bright 'spinner hubcaps.'

Such cars as this represented a culminating point in the history of American automobile design; the use of a car to project one's own character — or a character one would like to be — reached a high point, and then took a subtler, but no less bold, a turn in the 1960s. As early as the 1890s, however, car makers such as Frank Duryea were concerned with the public perception of their 'horseless buggies,' and sought to disguise the mechanical parts with side panels and the like. This book is a gallery of some of the cars that resulted when the twentieth century unleashed the automobile upon the American populace at large, and the reflection of public likes and dislikes — and designer's imaginations — created the cars that helped to define the American character from 1900 to 1969.

AT THE HEAD OF THE LINE

(1900–1920)

In the first two decades of our century, America's fascination with the gasoline-powered motorcar grew phenomenally. Steam and electric-powered cars ran a distant second — in the former case, it took too long to 'get up steam' in order to go anywhere; in the latter, the electric was slow, had to be recharged every 30 miles and lacked the styling flair that the internal combustion apparatus lent itself to. Even though such as the speedy Stanley Steamer lasted well into the 1920s, it was obvious by 1910 that the internal combustion engine was more convenient and reliable than either the electric or the steam powerplant.

Evidence for such determinations was often supplied by exhibitions and competitions. Manufacturers staged endurance runs and cross-country junkets to prove the reliability of their cars. Racing cars such as Henry Ford's famous '999' proved the mechanical acumen of the manufacturer, and added a cachet of speed and power to the makers' mark. It all helped to sell cars; and added greatly to the mystique of the automobile.

At first, Americans didn't trust a mechanical thing that had none of the nobleness, obvious symbolic value and just plain sense that horses had! But the machine went further and faster on its fuel than any horse could, and the motorcar clearly represented the future. The public soon reasoned that, since the horse was no longer 'out front,' something was missing. This led to the emplacement of false hoods on a number of mid-engine designs, and this in turn led to placing the engine itself up front, following in the footsteps of European styling in those early years. This engine-in-front configuration emulated the racing cars of the day, and it completed the replacement of the horse — as now the engine very clearly was the repository of the motorcar's 'horsepower.'

Popular automakers Oldsmobile, Cadillac, Oakland and Ford were emerging as the makers of quintessentially American automobiles covering the spectrum from the upper market to the low-price field, and were emblematic of an era that saw the US take the lead in car ownership and manufacture from the rest of the world. The upstart Chevrolet company was not long in setting up the design and manufacturing philosophy that would one day establish it as the world's leading automaker. Four of these companies were setting the stage for the massive, present-day General

Motors conglomerate, and Ford was establishing itself as one of the biggest automakers in the world.

American cars, though overall a bit more utilitarian, were quite in step with the best Europe had to offer, and in some cases, were leading the way. Luxury in automobiles became accepted as a symbol of the utmost prestige. Cadillac began a tradition of winning the 'Nobel Prize of automotive engineering,' Britain's Dewar Trophy, in 1909, for its parts standardization program (which inadvertently set the stage for Henry Ford's automobile assembly line).

The most common car design in the first decade was the runabout, a buckboard-like affair having its one-or-two cylinder engine located under the driver's seat — of which the Oldsmobile 'curved dash' models were among the most popular. Close on its heels in terms of popularity was the four-seat touring car, which enabled entire families to go on an outing in one vehicle. The closed car had not yet entered the average motorist's life; in the first years of our century, enclosed carbodies were expensive to build and cost premium prices; the first convenient compromise between open and closed cars was the foldable fabric top. Another stylistic advance was the low-slung, rakish 'gentleman's roadster' design, a racing car in street clothing, prime examples of which were the Stutz Bearcat and Mercer Raceabout, inveterate competitors of the second decade. Fenders became more rakish and the radiator was set behind the front axle a few inches, giving the front wheels an eager, thrusting appearance.

The Ford Model T appeared in 1908, and its long production run and low prices availed an auto for anyone who could afford a horse. In their 1984 book *Automania*, Julian Pettifer and Nigel Turner quote a rabidly pro-car newspaper editorial from the year 1915, which states, ' . . . with 20 million families, and only two million automobiles, we have got our national job one-tenth done. When every family has an automobile we can take some credit to ourselves.' The automobile had become a national project.

Above: The popular 1900–1904 Oldsmobile 'curved dash' (for better visibility) runabout, a seven horsepower automobile that could go 50 miles on five quarts of gasoline. Below is the scene just before the starting gun for the transcontinental race between two Oldsmobile runabouts, named as shown here, from New York City to Portland, Oregon, a total of 3890 miles, which opened the Lewis and Clark Centennial Exposition. *Old Scout* got there first, and the nation went wild over Oldsmobiles.

YOUR BEST BUSINESS PARTNER—the

OLDSMOBILE

Just consider: Low first cost, low operating expense, freedom from disorders, durability in service, easy and dependable control—six convincing facts demonstrated by the Oldsmobile. Will send you six times six convincing facts on your written request. Now it's up to you.

The Oldsmobile Standard Runabout, Model B—the car as indispensable to business economy as the telephone, the typewriter or the sewing machine—is now built with either straight or curved front. Its 7 h. p. single cylinder, water-cooled motor gives efficiency without complication. Price unchanged, $650.

The Oldsmobile Palace Touring Car, Model S—an American car, the product of American brains. Send for booklet telling why this four-cylinder 28 h. p. machine can give you more style, stability and **go for $2250** than any other car on the market at double the money.

The Double-Action Olds, Model L—the car with two working strokes to every revolution of the crank—is the **"proper"** thing in automobiles—the **talk** of the year. The absence of valves, guides, cams, and other intricacies attracts the novice—satisfies the expert. Its motor has only **three working parts.** It takes hills on high speed where other cars are forced into low gear. Its price with complete equipment, $1250. "Double-Action booklet" on request. It's good reading.

Member of Association Licensed Automobile Manufacturers.　　**OLDS MOTOR WORKS**　　*Canadian trade supplied from Canadian Factory, Packard Electric Co., Ltd., St. Catherines, Ont.*
　　　　　　　　　　　　　　　　Lansing, Mich., U. S. A.

Immediately above: An early advertisement for the Oldsmobile Standard Runabout, 'with either straight or curved front,' equating the importance of its development with that of the typewriter, telephone or sewing machine —all of which were new then! *At right and at top, above:* A 1910 Oldsmobile Limited. Times were changing, and the Oldsmobile line was gaining in sophistication. This majestic car was considerably more powerful and faster than the Runabout, and Limiteds of 1911 had huge, 707 cubic inch six cylinders for motive power, and could cruise easily at 60–70 mph! The 1910 Limited was immortalized in William H Foster's famous painting, *Setting the Pace*, the main theme of which was a record run by one of the fabulous New York Central Railroad express trains. A four cylinder, 40 horsepower 1912 Oldsmobile Autocrat Speedster averaged 60 mph for 265.44 miles in the Long Island Vanderbilt Cup race, and a decade earlier, in April, 1902, Ransom E Olds, in one of his Oldsmobiles, raced with Alexander Winton on the sands on Daytona Beach, both contestants' cars clocking 57 mph in the very first race at America's 'Birthplace of Speed.'

At the far left: The first Cadillac, a 1902 model, which was conceived in September of that year and brought out in October. The Detroit Automobile Company had reorganized as Cadillac Automobile Company; Henry Martyn Leland made sure that every Cadillac part was standardized and made to the precision of one thousandth of an inch, so that no reworking was needed to assemble a complete car. The first Cadillac, the Model A, resembled the Ford Model A, as Leland had input on both cars, but internally, the Ford and the Cadillac were radically different. *Below:* This luxurious 1912 Cadillac was the first car to use a self-starter, and had electric lighting and ignition as well. Cadillac's standardizing of parts had already won one Dewar Trophy for automotive excellence, and this model won the company another of the prestigious awards. Most cars of the era had crank starters, which could be dangerous when the engine coughed to life and the crank 'kicked back' in a contrarotation.

In 1899, when the first Oldsmobile was designed, Henry Ford founded the Detroit Automobile Company, which was to have made a line of cars that were low-priced, dependable and easy to maintain. These objectives proved more costly to develop than Ford's backers were willing to fund, so the company was sold, only to develop into Cadillac, one day to become America's foremost maker of luxury cars. Henry Ford did not give up: two racing victories by his cars (most notably, the world speed record holder '999,' driven by Barney Oldfield) in 1903 gave backers impetus to fund his projects, and soon he established the Ford Motor Company — the first engines he used were supplied by Horace and John Dodge. On these pages is the Ford Model A, the first of Ford Motor Company's many cars. This automobile had its horizontally-opposed two cylinder engine mounted under the front seat — notice the crank hole on the side of this car. Also standard was a two speed epicyclic gear box, the bulb horn and the carbide gas lamps which were in common use by autos of the era. Note the stowage basket by the rear seat here, and the cheerfully elegant visual harmony of orange, black and brass.

Main photo, these pages: The year was 1912, and Louis Chevrolet (standing, without a hat, at photo left), famous racing driver, had completed two years of developmental work on his first automobile. His mentor, WC Durant (standing at far right, wearing a derby) was the owner of Buick Motors and had founded the General Motors Company. Chevrolet's son and daughter-in-law share the front seat of this, the very first Chevrolet motorcar. This car was a six cylinder model, and first year production was 2999 vehicles; by 1916, this number had shot past 60,000 units! In the boxed photo, *right*, we see a 1913 Chevrolet. Note the leaf-spring front suspension and lack of front brakes, which was accepted practice.

These pages: An example of the world's most well-known vintage car, the Ford Model 'T.' The first Model Ts appeared at the British Motor Show and were a hit — 250 of the cars were sold on the spot. These had a top speed of 40 mph and a price of $850. Production of the Model T began on 1 October 1908, and ended in 1928, more than 15 million cars later. Model Ts were everywhere. The price of the car kept falling — all the way down to $260 in 1923, and the Ford Model T was literally *everywhere*.

The Model T gearbox was foot-operated: push the pedal down for low, let it up in the middle for neutral, and all the way up for high. A second pedal engaged reverse, and a third operated the transmission brake. It was a car said to be operable by anyone, and in 20 minutes, you'd be tooling down the road, pushing forward on the throttle lever to advance, and easing up to stop. Radiators were brass at first, but then to lower the price and sell even more cars, Ford made them out of sheet metal. Colors other than black were up to the buyer to arrange for himself. *Above:* A Model T and its successor (near), the Model A. *Below:* A 1913 Model T. *Below right:* A 1917 Model T.

These pages: A well-restored 1927 Ford Model T sedan. Henry Ford, realizing that the car's appeal would eventually wear out, shocked the world when he ordered production on the Model T to abruptly halt in 1928. His son Edsel was, soon enough, to temper his father's intense utilitarianism with an equally intense love of style (which would result in the creation of one of the great Ford products, the Lincoln Continental of the 1930s). Meanwhile, the 'Tin Lizzie,' as the Model T was affectionately called, just kept puttering along, distinctly unimpressive but 'reliable as the day is long,' as the slang of the period would have it. Oh, the Tin Lizzie had its quirks — some owners swore that the old gas buggies had real personalities!

Legends notwithstanding, the Model T was available in a variety of models, in any non-optional color — as the quote from Henry Ford goes — 'as long as it's black,' and was the car that introduced modern production line methods to the American auto industry. It was a simple, rugged and versatile machine, and there was *always* a Model T parts dealer nearby. The Model T was one of the most popular cars of all time, and it could be said to have brought the world at large into the automotive 20th century *en masse*, by dint of its ubiquity and easy maintenance. By sheer availability, the Ford Model T made of itself a *necessity*.

THE AMERICAN AUTO COMES OF AGE
(The 1920s)

The 1920s was a decade of phenomenal growth in the American auto industry; by 1929, the US manufactured 5.3 million cars, 10 times the entire production for the rest of the world: Packard, Chrysler, Chevrolet and Ford were watchwords around the world. The word 'style' was on everyone's lips, and when they said it, they meant the automobile.

Paint and auto finish was a major concern. Cars painted in bright hues in the early years faded after a year's wear and tear: this led to a trend of using only the more durable black paint (Henry Ford's paint of choice for his Model Ts). In the 1920s, General Motors invented Duco finish, which was long-lasting, dried faster, offered a wide range of pigments and kept its brilliance, too — even with such bright colors as blue, red and yellow. Two-or three-color auto paint schemes became common, and new stylistic horizons beckoned.

Previous to the 1920s, accessories were the province of a thriving and independent accessory industry. During the 1920s, manufacturers began to provide customers with accessories, and it wasn't long before wheel type, body color, upholstery, optional bumpers, spare tire covers, attachable rear trunks, radiator cap ornaments, cowl lights and molding were objects of selection when one ordered one's car.

Customers began to want more substantial-looking autos to give them the feeling of prestige that comes with 'having gotten a lot for your money.' The mid-1920s Chryslers were unusually low cars that yet retained a solidly conventional appearance. The Chrysler 'look' was gained via fat wheel spokes, large balloon tires and extra-deep fenders which emphasized a popular weighty appearance that was much imitated.

The Ford Model T accounted for 50 percent of all cars sold in the late teens and early 1920s. In 1924, however, General Motors brought out a true competitor in its redesigned Chevrolet, which cost $640 to the Ford's $525, but offered 'a touch of class.' While the Ford stratagem was based on buyer practicality, the Chevrolet stratagem was based on the buyers' emotions, and while the Chevy cost a bit more, with General Motors' then-newly developed installment plan, Ford's market share fell while Chevy's rose, even though Edsel Ford, Henry's son, influenced his father's stance on styling toward design upgrading on the old 'Tin Lizzie,' in 1925.

In 1920, the most popular car type was the phaeton, or touring car — a large, open car suitable for genteel outings — and was manufactured by almost all American makers, including Packard, Chrysler, Lincoln and Ford. In the mid-1920s, however, a resurgence in the unstable economy brought a renewed interest in the sporty roadster. The roadsters of the teens had a sprightly simplicity about them, being all-out speed machines; the new roadsters were heavier-looking and more stylized — thus, the speedy Stutz and the upstart Chrysler, among many other makes, appeared with the revised design, and their enlarged rear decks allowed the installation of the soon-to-be universal 'rumble seat' — so named for its rugged ride.

A major styling breakthrough occurred when, in 1921, the Essex

company produced a low-priced solution to the high cost of building closed carbodies, and the bulk of American manufacturers seized upon it; the closed car was made available to the masses. The closed car was good for all weather, with its openable windows and rain-proof construction. Eventually, closed cars would outsell all other configurations.

When famous personalities began buying their luxury cars from European makers, the American luxury car industry — temporarily asleep in a post-World War I isolationist funk — burst into a frenzy of indignant activity: they collaborated with such international custom body firms as Brewster, Rochambeau, De Causse and Fleetwood. Cadillac hired a custom body builder named Harley Earl, and made him head of their own, in-house custom body shop: soon, custom innovations entered the production line.

Following in the styling footsteps of the luxury cars were such high-priced popular makes as Chrysler and Lincoln, and in *their* footsteps followed the low-priced cars that offered the common man a variety of models. In the 1920s, America became a country of the automobile. This was not accomplished by the luxury cars; quite the opposite, it was the common, working-class automobile — the Chevrolet, the Dodge and others, led by the venerable Model T — that put America 'in the driver's seat.'

In 1909, the Oakland Motor Car Company joined Oldsmobile and Buick under the umbrella of General Motors. The company had been producing cars for two years previous to this. Oakland produced fine automobiles, and was a pillar of the General Motors Company into the 1920s. During model year 1925, Oakland had exclusive use of the then-new Duco Satin Finish enamel paint, and its first use was on the 'True Blue' Oakland Six *(below left)* of that year. The next year, a new product line saw light under the Oakland aegis, this was the new, low-priced Pontiac Six, and was advertised as 'The Chief of the Sixes.' This car was available in two models, a two passenger coupe and a five passenger coach body, with a 40 horsepower, 186.5 cubic inch six cylinder having the shortest stroke length of any engine of the period. It proved to be a very popular car, and in 1930, Pontiac's six cylinder outsold the then-new Oakland V-8; in 1932, the Oakland company was renamed the Pontiac Motor Company. *Above right:* The first Pontiac, a 1926 model. *Below:* Another 1926 Pontiac. Note the distinctive Indian head hood ornament, which, in various configurations, would be the Pontiac emblem for decades.

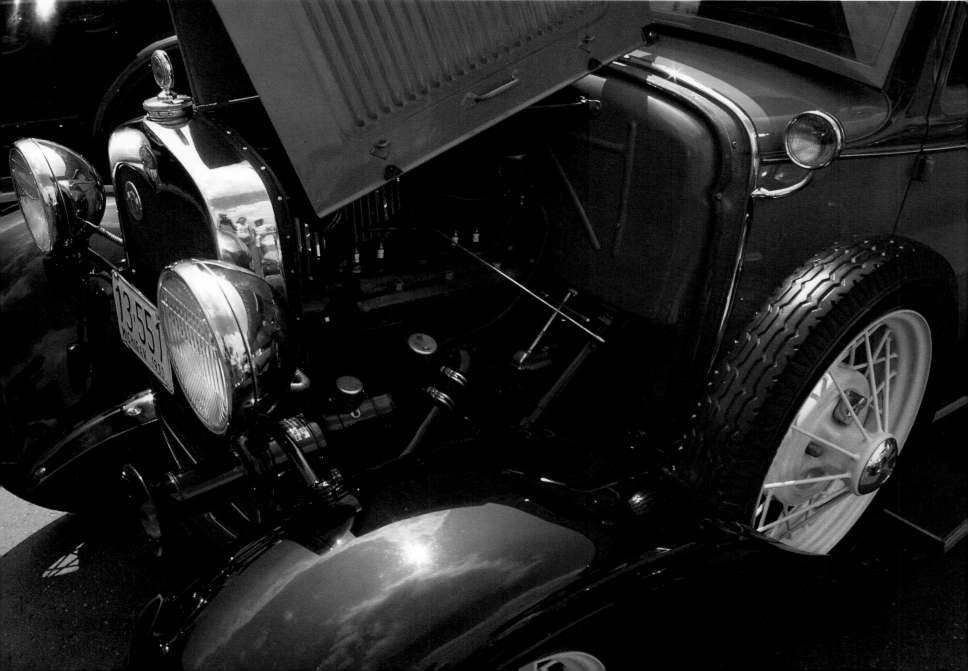

When he shut down the Model T production line, Henry Ford took six months to produce his new model (with an old designation), the Ford Model A *(these pages)*. This had a 40 horsepower four cylinder, a three-speed transmission, four-wheel mechanical brakes and was capable of 62 mph. The car was available in a variety of models, and Ford established factories in England and Germany to avoid import duties, and the Ford factory in Cologne was the most advanced European auto factory of the 1930s. As soon as Ford brought out the Model A, Chevrolet brought out a six cylinder competitor at no extra cost, and the Model A was discontinued in 1932, however, this same year saw the birth of the Model B/18, with the revolutionary new Ford flathead V-8 — an engine that would set records and win races for the next 20 years.

These pages: A 1929 Model A roadster, with stowable convertible top and rumble seat open (in the 1930s, Americans would rename the rumble seat the more genteel 'rear deck seat'). The Model A four cylinder, a side-valve engine that was good enough for its day, could not fend off the market competition from the Chevrolet six. Like most Ford engines, this was a powerplant that could absorb a a lot of punishment. If it was not particularly powerful, it was durable, and its design laid the experiential background for the flathead Ford Y-block V-8, which appeared in 1932 with the Model B — and was the Ford mainstay well into the 1950s. The main pleasure of the Model A, especially roadsters such as the one shown here, was the simple assurance that here was a stylish yet simple automobile that would reliably get you where you wanted to go.

Stutz built its first Bearcat in 1914—a 397.4 cubic inch four cylinder car that developed 60 horsepower and won a lot of races. In the 1920s, Stutz kept up the Bearcat name and developed another famous racer, the Blackhawk. With a distinctive sporty look and overhead cam engines, the Stutz name stood for performance and a dashing style. *Below and upper right:* Two views of a 1928 Stutz roadster. *Above:* A 1923 Bearcat.

Above: A 1928 Franklin. Franklins had air-cooled engines and laminated ash frames, and had a suspension that could negotiate rough roads 20 mph faster than anything else on wheels. In 1928, Chryslers came in third and fourth at Le Mans. *Below* is a 1928 Imperial 80 Club Coupe. *At right:* Dodge came under the Chrysler umbrella the same year that this 1928 Dodge Victory Six was produced.

CAR NO. _____

CLASS NO. _____

YR.   MAKE   OWNER

The fabulous Lincoln. Henry Leland, the man who bought Henry Ford's first company and turned it into Cadillac in the earliest years of this century, founded the Lincoln Company in 1917, and when the company had financial problems in 1922, Henry Ford bought the company, in a very fortuitous turnabout. Henry turned the newly bought company over to his son Edsel.

MICHIGAN 1928
773·749

The Imperial was Chrysler's top-of-the line auto, and for those who owned Imperials, the feeling of sitting in the cockpit and taking the wheel in hands was indeed a royal sensation. These were finely machined, superbly turned out cars, and with your Chrysler Imperial six cylinder purring away under the hood, you felt that you were at least the 'King of the Road.' *At immediate left* is an overview of the passenger/driver compartment of a 1926 Imperial 80 coupe. Note the famous radiator cap way out in front, and the richly upholstered seats.

Of course, driving one of Chrysler's standard roadsters was a pleasure, too, and the Chrysler's narrow-shell 'ribbon' radiator — brought out in 1929 — was widely imitated in Europe. *At far left and below:* Two views of a 1929 Chrysler roadster, with obligatory 'rumble seat' closed. Note the clean, classic American roadster lines of this car, pointed up all the more by the large grill, which is, of course, of the sensational narrow-shell 'ribbon' type which Chrysler made so popular. Brakes on this car were, for the first time in a Chrysler model year, of the internal-expansion caliper type. The powerplant was, of course, a six cylinder of the type which Chrysler took to LeMans the year before and placed an astonishing third and fourth behind the much more highly touted Bentley and Stutz cars.

LUXURY MEETS THE STREAMLINED FAMILY CAR

(1930 – 1942)

It was an escapist entertainment for some of the masses, and a galling irony to others, to observe those who had not suffered the ravages of the Stock Market Crash driving around in cars that, for sheer wealth of material and exquisite design, were breathtaking, and breathtakingly expensive. The new Auburns, Cords, Duesenbergs, Packards, Cadillacs, Pierce-Arrows and other luxury cars seemed to be even more exquisite and powerful, and fueled more dreams than ever before. But new styling frontiers were presented by less costly models.

It was a major styling advance when the 1931 REO Royale Eight introduce its rounded corners and smooth windshield 'brow,' to critical and public acclaim. The 1932 Graham Eight went even further, and established the styling of the next few years by bringing the front fenders down almost even with the bumper and wrapping them around behind the front wheels to cover the chassis. The grille was sloped gently forward at the bottom and blended into the splash pan, creating a smooth, harmonious symphony of components that would be widely copied.

Prestigious Pierce-Arrow got into the swing of things with its radical, streamlined Silver Arrow showcar, which featured fenders that were semi-blended into the carbody, but the real news of the mid-1930s in terms of streamlining was the Chrysler Airflow, a car that not only melded body and fenders, but body and frame as well, creating a rigid unit that showed advances in chassis/body design. The Airflow also redistributed automobile weight — from the traditional 60 rear/40 front percentage to a new and startling 45 rear/55 front, solving the old problem of rear seat comfort, by placing rear seat passengers ahead of the rear axle for a better ride altogether. This also shoved the radiator well ahead of the front wheels, giving the car a comparatively front-heavy appearance that was actually the wave of the future, but in the Airflow was accentuated to an unfortunate degree by the car's bulbous nose.

While the Airflow was a good-handling and riding car overall, its front end had to be disguised by the addition of a new hood. Ironically, the car's 'fastback' rear end was widely copied, and in the following years, its enclosed trunk with increased luggage space and spare tire stowage, comfortable rear seating arrangement and other advances were incorporated

into other designs, such as that of Pontiac and other mid-price cars in 1936. The streamline program was heavily imitated by Ford's prestigious Lincoln models from 1936 onwards.

Another breakthrough in auto design occurred with General Motors' practice of 'trickle down design,' which was begun in the early 1930s. Typically, the top-of-the-line Cadillac would pioneer a luxury design feature, and one or two years later, lower-priced General Motors lines like Chevrolet would 'inherit' the design feature to a greater or lesser extent, creating a 'family resemblance' among General Motors cars. This, too, was to see much imitation in the years that followed.

Grilles became narrower — now that they were essentially separated from the radiator, grille size and shape did not affect cooling capacity; the old, lash-on wooden luggage trunks disappeared in lieu of modern 'streamlined' built-in trunks. Driver vision reached a crisis in the late 1930s, with windows shrinking almost to view-slits before manufacturers heeded complaints and criticism, and began making larger windows.

The grand cars of the Great Depression — Packard, Auburn, Duesenberg, Cord, Pierce-Arrow — fared badly in an unstable business climate which dictated that only the most well-funded should survive, and the much-in-demand family cars — Pontiac, Chevrolet, Ford, Dodge and others — were here to stay. A few luxurious cars survived, though — Cadillac, with hardy General Motors behind it, and Packard, though having had a traumatic time of it, and Chrysler's offerings. And a new luxury car was introduced- — Ford's Lincoln Continental, which came into being at the same time that Erret Cord's Auburn-Cord-Duesenberg empire was crumbling. The Continental was a new kind of car for the rich, with its sensational combination of roadster, luxury car and streamlined elements; it was lauded on its inauguration. The ideal look of the American car had gone from the broad radiator and rectilinear, monumental surfaces of Cadillac's stunning V-16 models of the early 1930s to the sloping, faired-in configurations of the early 1940s. In combination with the consolidations, however, America was rediscovering the broad body surface, which would lead to the future.

Back in the first decade of this century, Packard began its tradition of being among the most exclusive elite of American luxury cars. That

massive, trademark radiator visually communicated a tradition of excellence that saw Packard's dominance from 1910 into the 1930s, when manufacture of lower-priced cars sullied the line's 'exclusivity.' Powered by a massive straight eight or an even more impressive V-12, the Packard lineage set a standard which none exceeded, and only a few approached.

These pages: A selection of early 1930s Packards — a lineup of the utmost in classic American automotive luxury.

These pages: A 1933 Packard V-12 touring car, with 160 bhp and coachwork by the finest, which was common for top-of-the-line Packards. Not only were they beautiful to look at, they drove like dreams, and possessed a stateliness that is simply unavailable in automobiles today. Note the swan on the radiator cap, the visual echo created by the rims of chrome on the spare tire cover, which are echoed once more in the beauty rings and hubcaps on the wheels. Everywhere you look, there is loving, tasteful and elegant attention to detail, none of it overdone, everything is in exact proportion to create the look of an incredibly well-crafted object. And that paint job! No modern design would survive it!

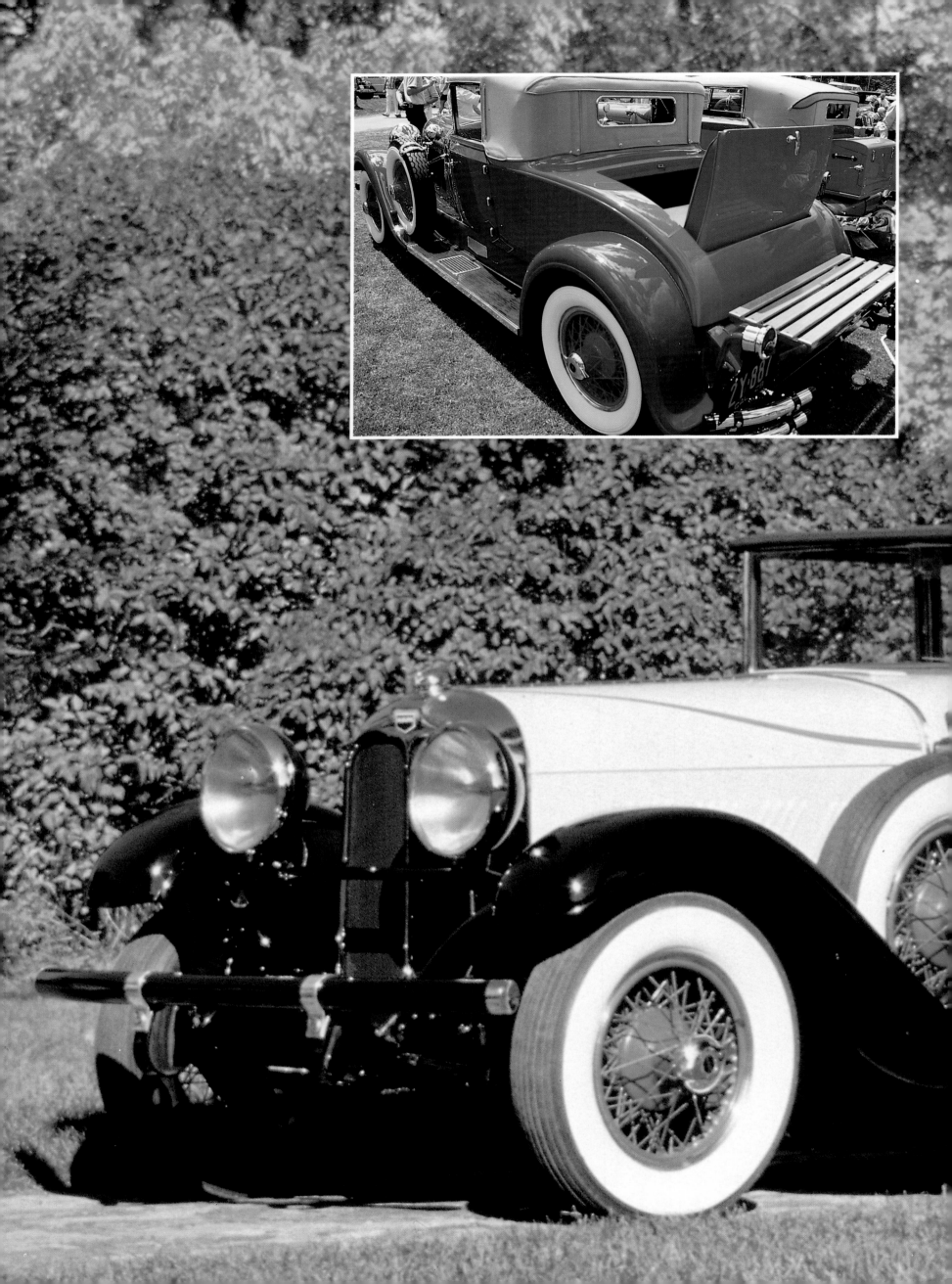

In 1924, Erret Cord took over control of the Auburn Company, and by 1930, he had created a legendary line of cars, including the fabulous Auburn 120 Speedster, and had a conglomerate enterprise under whose aegis not only the elegant and speedy Auburn was produced, but also the eponymous Cord Motor Company and the grandest of all grand American automotive ventures, the mighty Duesenberg. Cord controlled Lycoming Motors in Pennsylvania, and he equipped his new Auburns with a brand new, freshly designed, high performance Lycoming straight eight. The Speedster was to hold many world's records, and as the 1930s wore on, was to become even more powerful. The entire line of Auburns was held in esteem by a public who sought speed, elegance, and lightness of line.

At left and far left: A turn-of-the-1930s Auburn roadster: note that, in the near photo, the front end of a 12-cylinder Auburn boattail roadster is also visible just beyond the nearer car. *Below:* A 1930 Auburn town car, with a Lycoming straight eight under its engine bonnet.

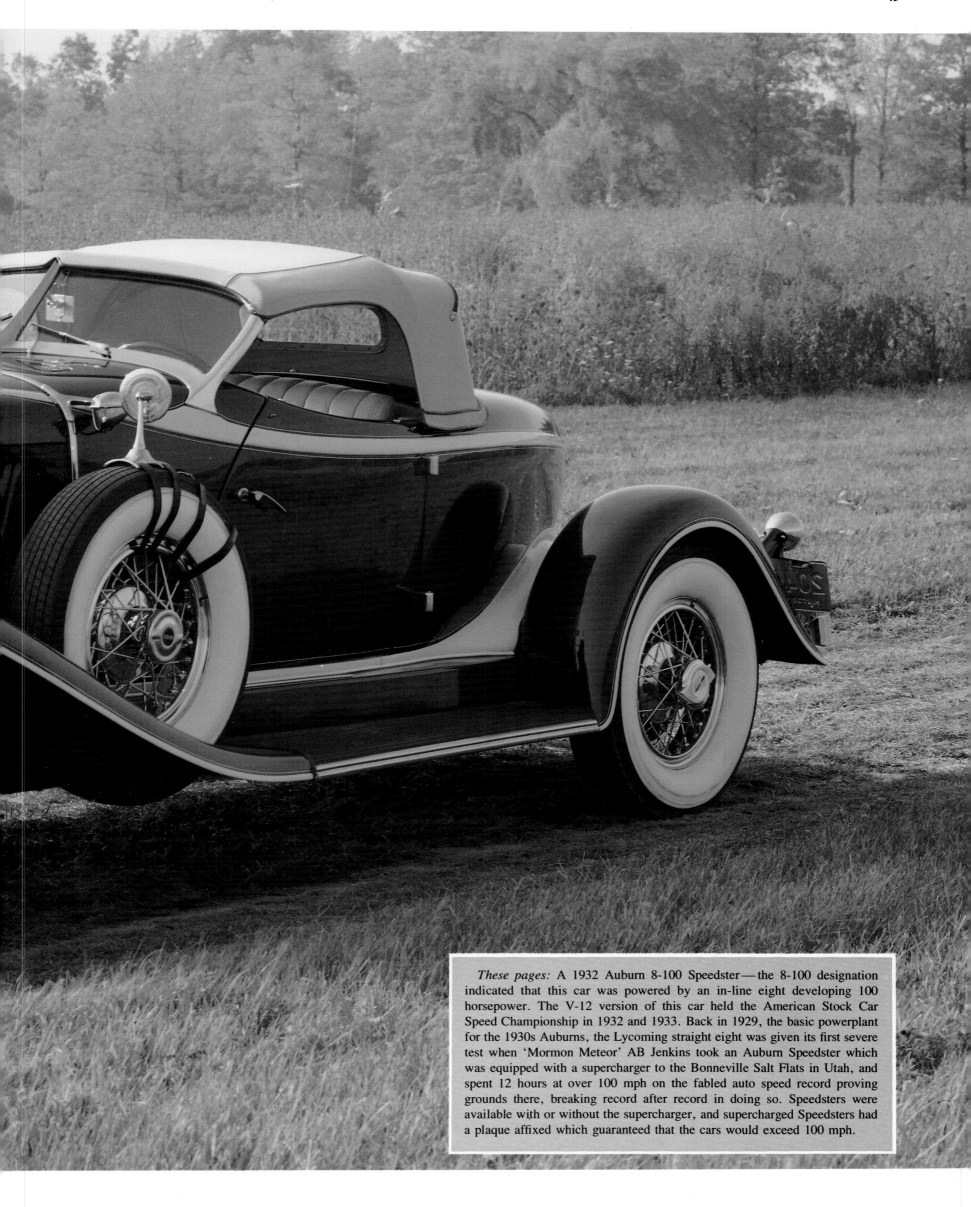

These pages: A 1932 Auburn 8-100 Speedster—the 8-100 designation indicated that this car was powered by an in-line eight developing 100 horsepower. The V-12 version of this car held the American Stock Car Speed Championship in 1932 and 1933. Back in 1929, the basic powerplant for the 1930s Auburns, the Lycoming straight eight was given its first severe test when 'Mormon Meteor' AB Jenkins took an Auburn Speedster which was equipped with a supercharger to the Bonneville Salt Flats in Utah, and spent 12 hours at over 100 mph on the fabled auto speed record proving grounds there, breaking record after record in doing so. Speedsters were available with or without the supercharger, and supercharged Speedsters had a plaque affixed which guaranteed that the cars would exceed 100 mph.

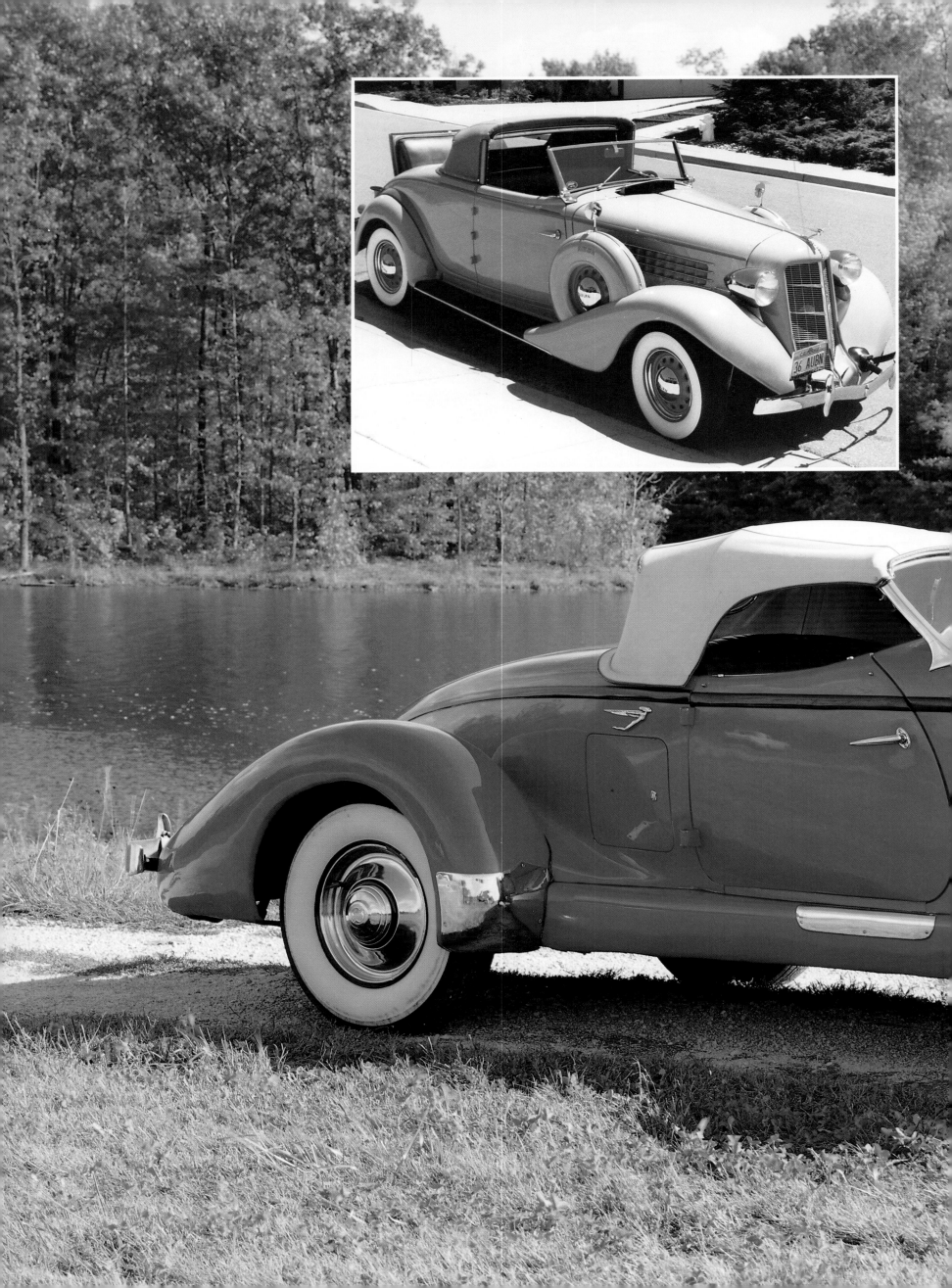

Below: The fabled 1935 Auburn Type 851 boattail Speedster, designed by Gordon Buehrig. This very elegant car was powered by a Switzer-Cummins supercharged Lycoming straight eight developing 150 bhp at 4000rpm, and could exceed 100 mph with ease. *At left:* Two views of a 1936 Auburn Cabriolet, with Palm Beach tan body and orange trim and wheels. Its originality is certified by the Auburn-Cord-Duesenberg Club, and was originally purchased in 1936, at Spokane, Washington. The car was restored by Jack L Hanson, of Spokane. The car is owned by Mr Al A Samolis of Danville, California, and is the only 1936 Auburn Cabriolet in the United States.

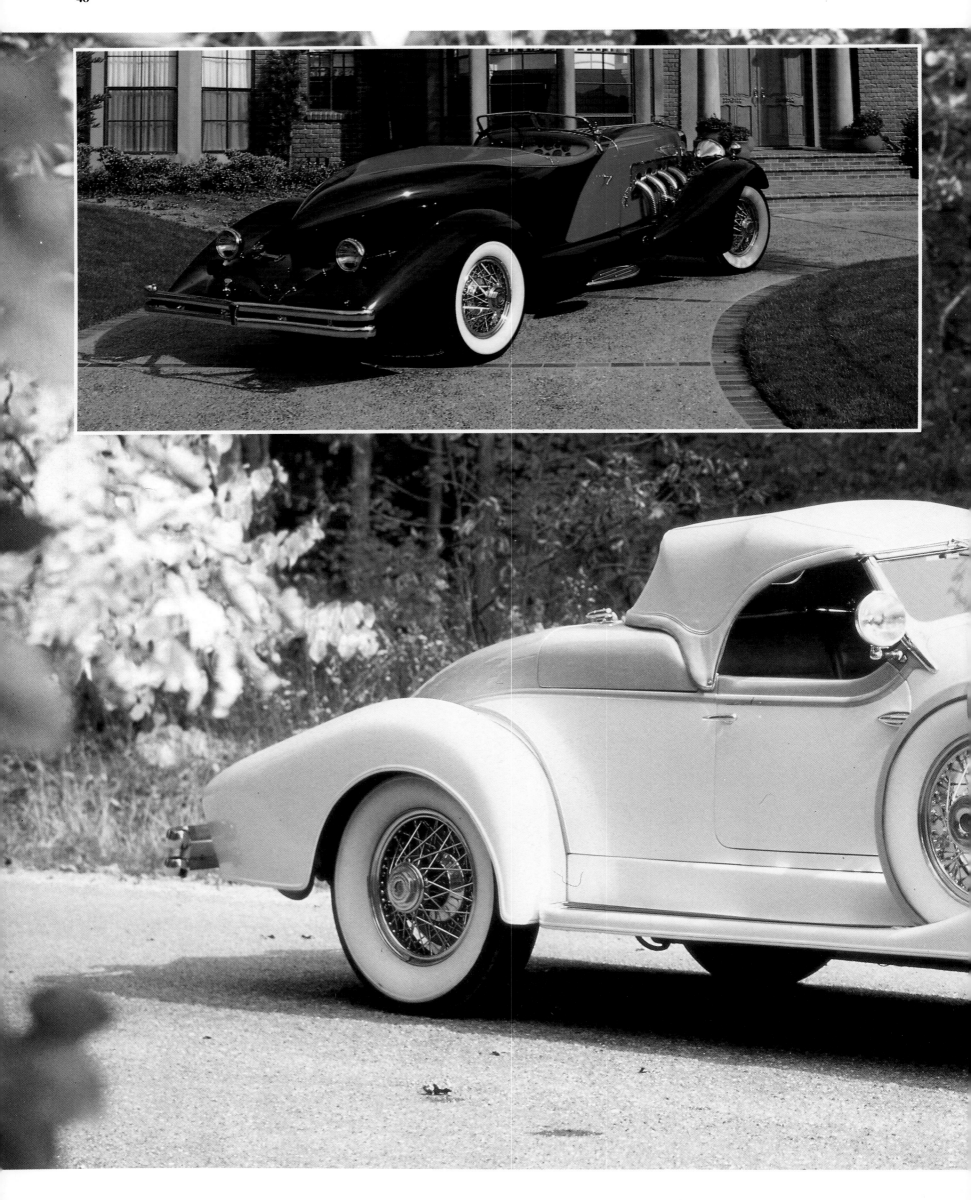

There was no other car to compare with this one, the mighty Duesenberg. The Duesenberg brothers began building racing cars in the teens of this century, and soon enough, their cars' tremendous success gave rise to series of road cars. The Duesenbergs were short on financial expertise, however, and there came the time when Duesenberg entered Erret Cord's automotive stables. Cord set about designing better-looking bodies for the Duesenbergs' impeccable mechanical plants, and the finest car ever built in the United States was the result. In 1929, the first of the Duesenbergs of the line's 'golden age' came out. This was billed as 'The World's Finest Car,' with its freshly-designed 422 cubic inch Lycoming straight eight under its distinctively lengthy engine bonnet. This car had 265 bhp, twice that of any other American car, and was capable of 116 mph with ease. Much use of aluminum was made, and the engine was rubber-mounted in a very rigid frame. With hydraulic brakes on all four wheels and variable servo assist for these, the car was also possessed of an amazing, uncompromising, luxuriously rakish look.

The Duesenbergs of the 1930s expounded upon this basic theme with the finest coach bodywork money could buy, and the cost of one model was, just as its nomenclature had it, 'Twenty Grand.' In 1932, the ultimate Duesenberg was produced — this was the astonishing Duesenberg SJ, which was equipped with a centrifugal supercharger for a power boost to 320 bhp and a top speed of 130 mph. The supercharger eliminated the possibility of routing the exhaust tubes under the engine bonnet, so an even more sporting touch was given to the car's appearance by the addition of huge, chromed exterior exhaust tubes protruding from the sides of the 'hood.' Two extra-short chassis models were produced for Hollywood personalities, and one of these belonged to Clark Gable. The cars came equipped with an automatic chassis lubrication device which did its duty every several thousand miles and a full range of sophisticated and sometimes overbearingly helpful instrumentation.

With the demise of Erret Cord's auto empire in 1937, the Duesenberg, Cord and Auburn lines were no longer produced, though there have been attempts to resurrect the makes from time to time, with little success. Perhaps what befits such legends is just that they remain legends! *At left:* A very extroverted Duesenberg SJ boattail roadster. *Below:* A very elegant 1933 SJ boattail — a glimpse of the finest.

These pages: A 1937 Cord 812 Berline — yet another product of the fertile genius of Erret Cord, whose Auburn-Cord-Duesenberg automobile conglomerate was a virtual 'General Motors' of fabulous automobiles. Of any line of cars in the annals of American motoring, the Cord, whose production life for all makes and models lasted from 1929–1937, was probably the one with the most pervasive mystique. The very look of models such as the Berline shown here was and still is enough to stimulate one to wonder what it might be like to sit behind the wheel and look out over that long hood, and feel the front wheels pull you like an obedient team of horses as that huge Lycoming eight emits its assuring rumble.

The first Cord was designed by Carl Van Ranst, who had worked with Harry Miller on the front-wheel drive racing cars that had dominated the Indianapolis track since 1926. This new automobile bearing Erret Lobban Cord's name was the L-29, which bore resemblance to the Duesenberg 'look,' and was powered by the same engine as the Auburn 120.

Introduced in 1935, the second Cord was the famous 810, which probably has influenced more conceptions of the Cord motorcar than any other model, with its headlights that could be cranked down to 'disappear' into the fronts of its fenders. This model was also known as the 'coffin nose' Cord. The de Dion front axle used on the L-29 was replaced on the 810 with independent front suspension. This was an automotive first for America. The chassis and body formed a rigid unit, and the transmission was fitted with an ingenious pre-selector, in which a miniature gear lever on the steering column moved in a selector gate.

The Cord 935 of 1936 was a little more standard-looking, with its vertical grille as opposed to the horizontal louvers of the 810. The 935 did, however, also have the 'hideaway' headlights. The Cord 812, with its huge external exhaust tubes, was introduced in 1937, but by then the Cord saga was almost over. For the record, though, the 812 was the Cord that most enthusiasts seek.

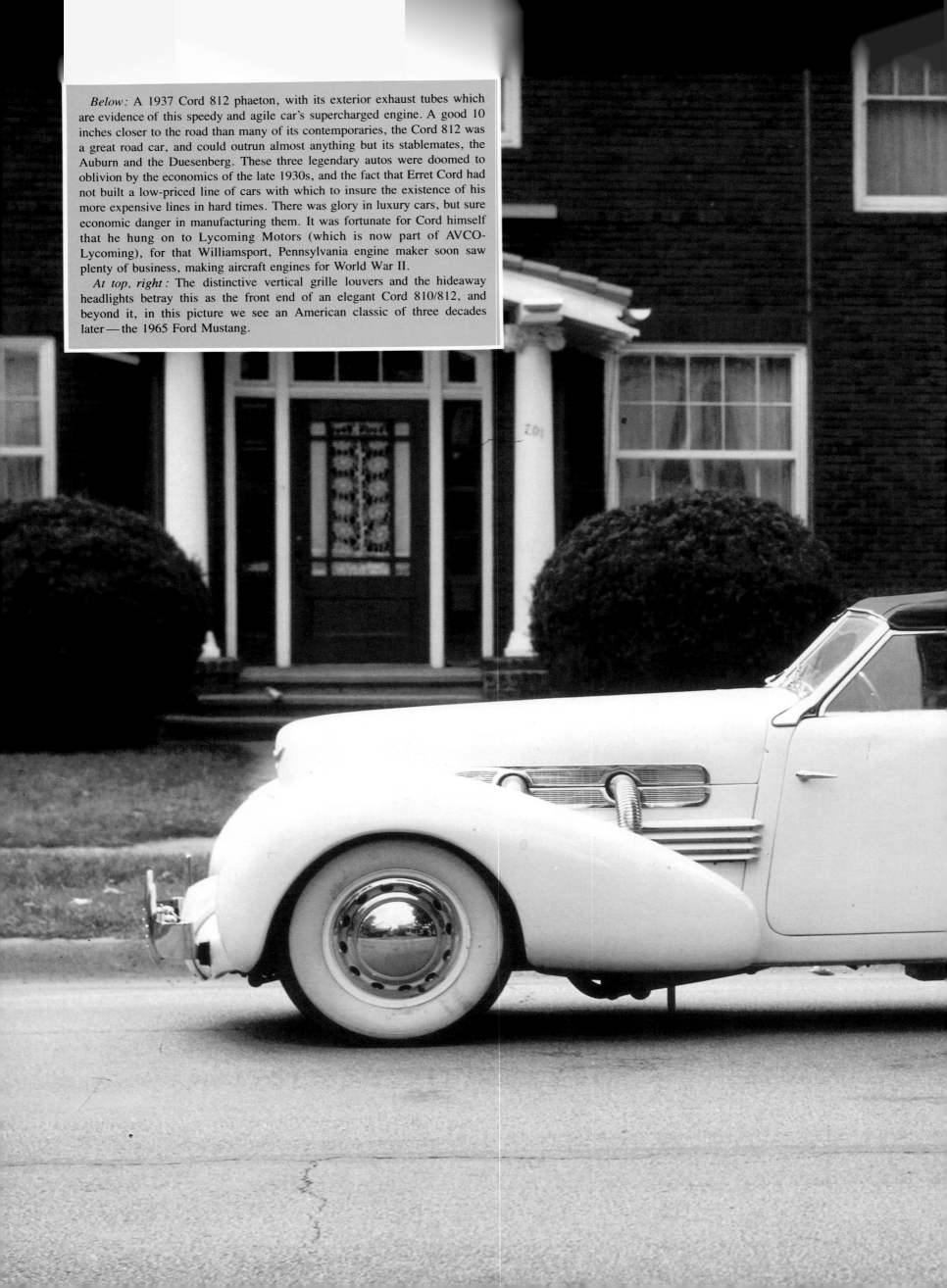

Below: A 1937 Cord 812 phaeton, with its exterior exhaust tubes which are evidence of this speedy and agile car's supercharged engine. A good 10 inches closer to the road than many of its contemporaries, the Cord 812 was a great road car, and could outrun almost anything but its stablemates, the Auburn and the Duesenberg. These three legendary autos were doomed to oblivion by the economics of the late 1930s, and the fact that Erret Cord had not built a low-priced line of cars with which to insure the existence of his more expensive lines in hard times. There was glory in luxury cars, but sure economic danger in manufacturing them. It was fortunate for Cord himself that he hung on to Lycoming Motors (which is now part of AVCO-Lycoming), for that Williamsport, Pennsylvania engine maker soon saw plenty of business, making aircraft engines for World War II.

At top, right: The distinctive vertical grille louvers and the hideaway headlights betray this as the front end of an elegant Cord 810/812, and beyond it, in this picture we see an American classic of three decades later — the 1965 Ford Mustang.

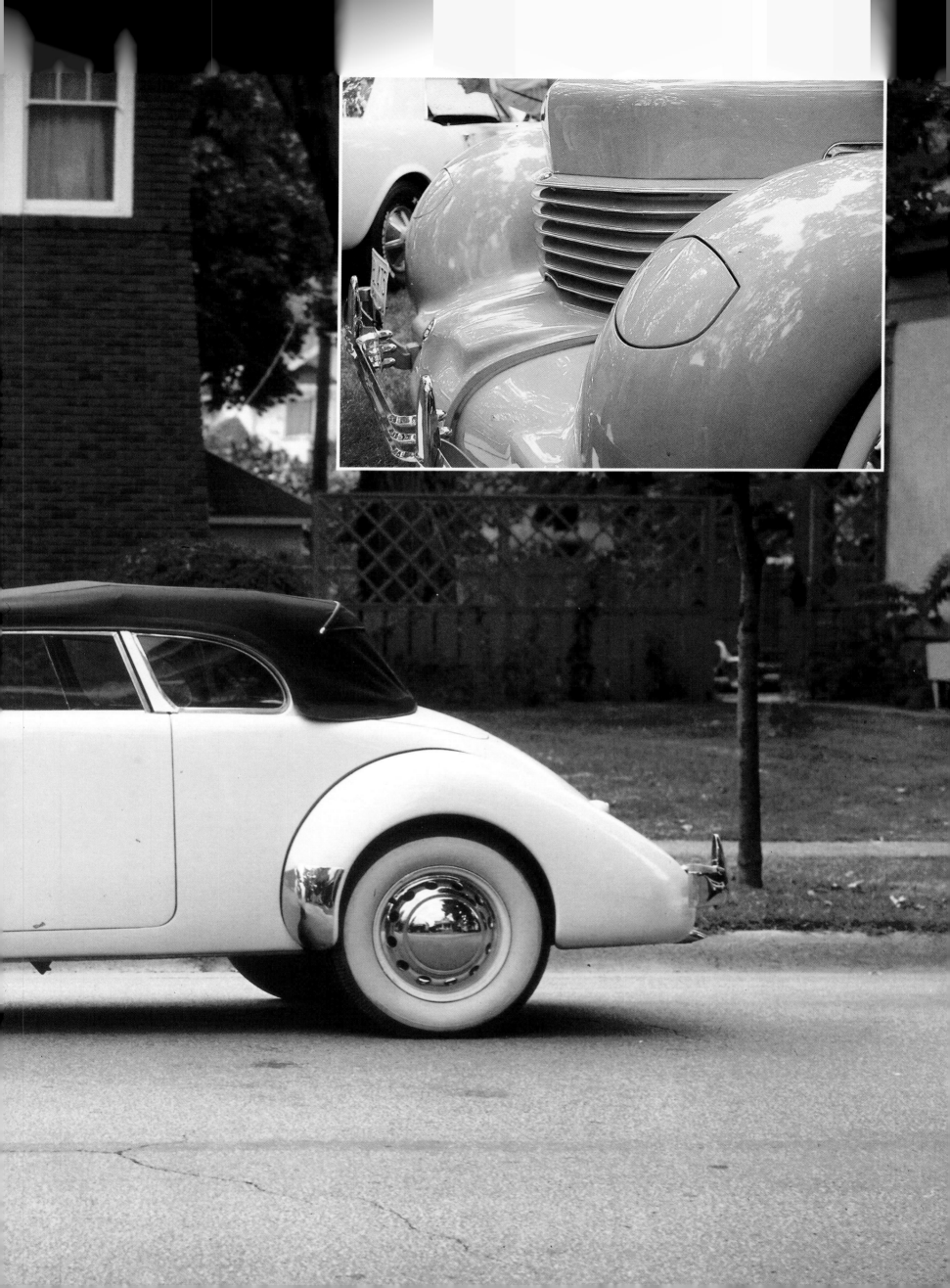

Lincoln rose from being one of the famous police cars of the 1920s to being a paragon of luxury in the 1930s. *Above and above far right:* Views of a finely-restored 1931 Lincoln roadster, evidencing the increased, 145-inch wheelbase which was introduced that year. All Lincolns were subject to rigorous testing before they left the factory, and were of a standard of finish equal to any car in the world. Yet the Lincoln incorporated many Ford ideas, such as interchangeability of parts between old and new models (within limits). In the 1930s, all Lincolns came equipped with a larger Lincoln side-valve V-8 engine, the standard mode of Lincoln power since 1920. In 1932, Lincoln introduced a V-12 — unique for any but the most expensive auto makes. Lincoln top models KA and KB had tolerance specifications of between 1/5000 and 1/10,000 of an inch. In 1934, the 414 cubic inch V-12 Lincoln Model K replaced them, and the legendary V-12 (269 cubic inches) Lincoln Zephyr was introduced.

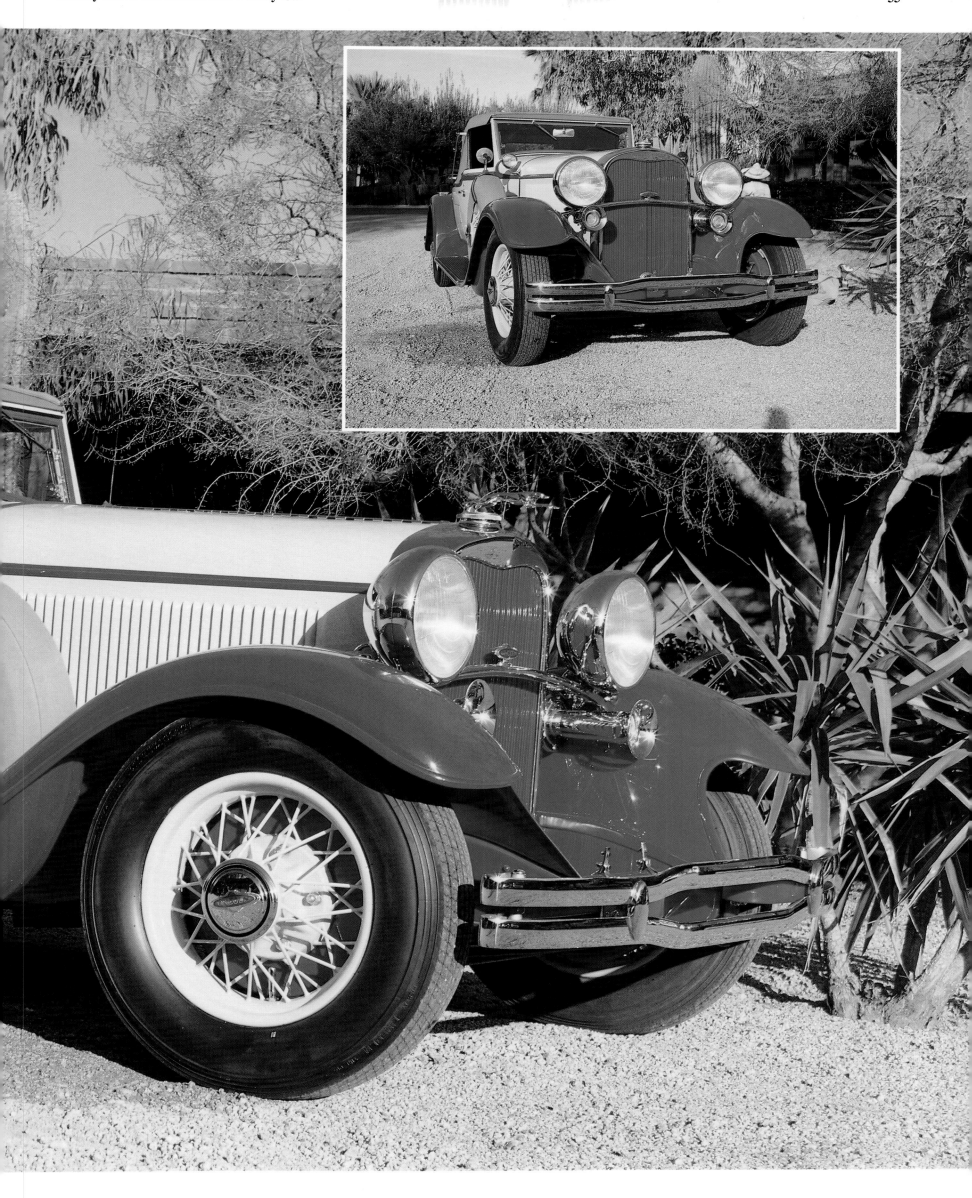

At right: A 1930 Cadillac. This model was equipped with the Cadillac invention of 1928, the synchronized-shifting 'Synchro-Mesh' transmission. In 1930, Cadillac introduced a V-12 model, and vacuum-servo-assist brakes were available on the larger Cadillac models in 1932. The entire line changed over to hydraulic brakes in 1937. Much of this was the product of Cadillac engineering genius Ernest Seaholm. Seen below is the embodiment of Ernest Seaholm's proudest achievement, the 1930 Cadillac Model 452, the world's first V-16 powered production car. The overhead valve system in this ultra-smooth engine was extraordinarily quiet, thanks to hydraulic valve lifters. This powerplant developed 165 horsepower from 452 cubic inches. The advent of the V-16 was indeed a 'shining moment.'

At far left: A 1932 Chrysler touring car. *At immediate left and below:* Two views of an impeccable 1933 Chrysler. For an auto that is not generally counted worthy of being in the ranks of the Auburn, Duesenberg, Packard and Pierce-Arrow, you can detect an astonishing attention to detail on this car. Styling in the early 1930s Chrysler was definitely influenced by the Auburns and Duesenbergs of 1929–31, especially in the gentle 'vee' of the radiator, even though the trademark Chrysler narrow-shell 'ribbon' radiator had caught on around the world. In 1931, two new straight eights — of 385 cubic inches and 125 horsepower; and 238 cubic inches and 80 horsepower——were offered in addition to existing engines. Chrysler also introduced 'Floating Power' engine mountings, and automatic clutches and freewheels in 1932, plus a version of the synchronized transmission in 1933 and automatic overdrive in 1934. Chrysler was always researching new ways, new methods and new means of doing things, and the years ahead would show that all the research paid off, with a few exceptions. For example, the 1930 Chrysler was the first American car to have a radio as an option.

These pages: As can be seen by these views of a 1932 Chrysler Le Baron Model CH Roadster, Chrysler was right in step with the latest in elegant design in the early 1930s. This particular car was first owned by Walter P Chrysler II, who no doubt drove his family's product with a good deal of justifiable pride. Chrysler advances continued through the years, with independent front suspension being adopted in 1937, and steering column-mounted gear shift and Chrysler 'fluid drive' appearing in 1939. The Chrysler Corporation included Chrysler, De Soto, Dodge and Plymouth, and was the third-largest American manufacturer after Ford and General Motors.

Despite the unsuccessful Airflow line, Chrysler was America's second largest auto seller, after General Motors, from 1933–1950.

Note how the roadster on these pages successfully imitates much of the traditional 'boattail' look without actually *being* a boattail, and how the car's low windshield, long hood and substantial grillwork give the impression of solidity, grace and power. Compare these views with those of the Auburns, Cords and Duesenbergs shown previously. This car was powered by the top-of-the-line 385 cubic-inch Chrysler Imperial straight eight engine, which developed 125 horsepower.

These pages: A 1930 Pierce-Arrow coupe. Pierce-Arrow is still linked with the utmost in American luxury car manufacture, more than 50 years after the company's demise in 1938. The company temporarily merged with Studebaker in the 1920s — but the manufacture of its high-quality autos continued unabated. A number of speed trials with new engines in the 1930s seemed likely to drown the competition — in 1932, the new Pierce-Arrow V-12 made its appearance, and 'Mormon Meteor' AB Jenkins drove a modified version of the new Pierce-Arrow to a 24-hour speed record of 112.97 mph unofficially, and shortly thereafter set an official 24-hour speed record of 117 mph with a stock Pierce-Arrow. He then set another such record of 127.2 mph with a slightly modified Pierce-Arrow. The company introduced the legendary Silver Arrow model in 1933.

CALIFORNIA
2AGP855

You can tell by the incredibly snobbish glamour—as well as by the unmistakable hood ornaments—that the cars shown on these pages are Pierce Arrows. *At left* is a 1933 sedan, and *above* are two 1930 models—a touring car and a sedan—with different paint and grille treatments. Pierce-Arrow stood for snob appeal, but like many independednt manufacturers, could not survive the rigors of the 1930s. The last Pierce-Arrows, Models 1601–03 offered huge vacuum-servo brakes, quadruple headlamps, tinted safety glass, crankcase emission control—and true luxuriousness.

These pages: The archer on the radiator cap of this elegant Pierce-Arrow roadster still kneels, poised to let his shaft fly, and the exquisitely crafted, powerful automobile that carries him so haughtily aloft will surely provide him all the speed and confidence with which to catch that very same arrow! The marvellous 368 cubic inch Pierce-Arrow straight eight of 1929 led to the V-12s of the 1930s, and these newly-developed engines ranged from 397 cubic inches to 431 cubic inches, and there was a prototype of a huge 464 cubic inch V-12 which had been tested in the mid-1930s.

The V-12 was an excellent powerplant, strong and supremely smooth — plus, it was simply hard to beat the confident, deep throated rumble of a V-12 when it came to impressing the superiority of one's motorcar upon the populace at large.

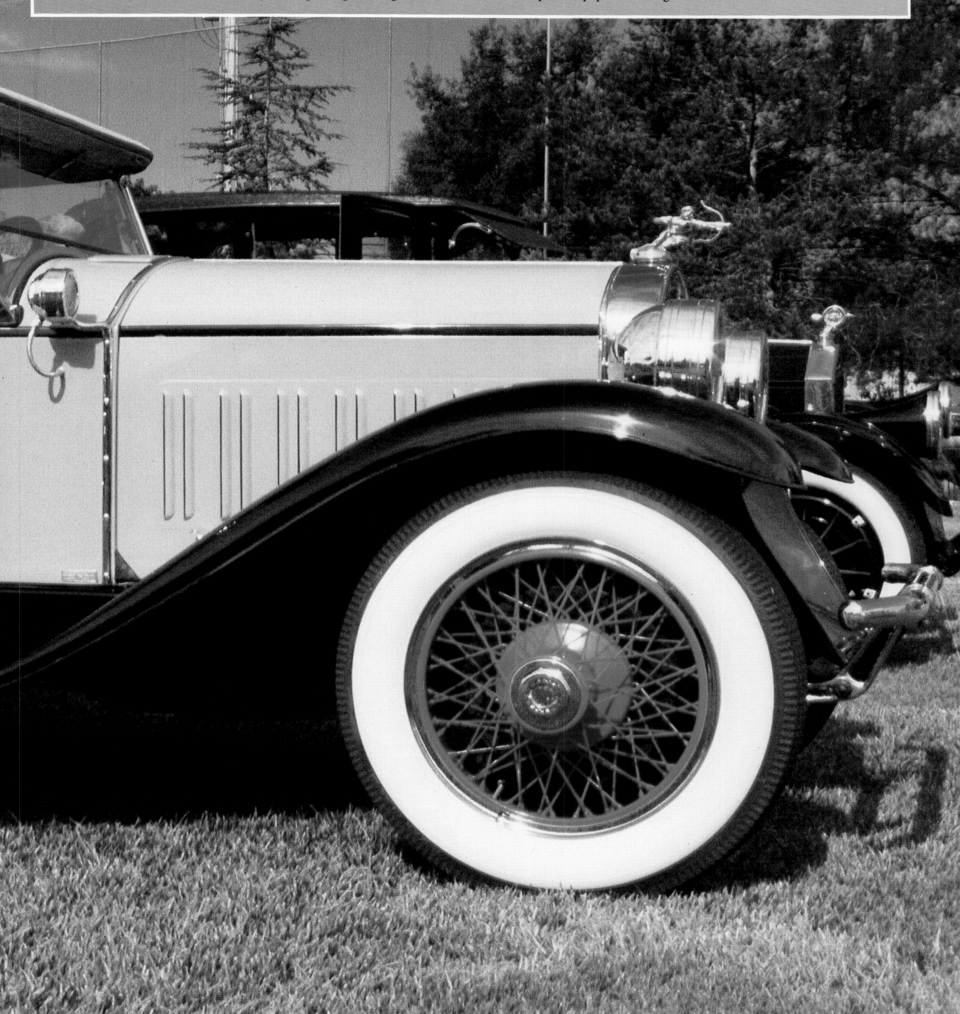

Above, on this page, is a 1930 American Austin roadster. This car belongs to M Josephine Shannon of Monterey Park, California. *Above opposite:* A Whippet Model 96 coupe, a four cylinder car of 32 horsepower, which belongs to Manuel and Adele Fortes of Redwood City, California.

Main photo: Three Pontiacs. Left to right, a 1934 roadster; a 1930 coupe and a 1932 sedan. In 1930, Pontiac sported a 210 cubic inch six, and in 1932 the first Pontiac eight appeared.

These pages: While the quiet, smooth and powerful Cadillac V-16 was a tremendous fad, and the ideal luxury car engine, the tried and true V-8 still had a place in the hearts of Cadillac owners. This engine had served the line well for over a decade at the point the car on these pages was manufactured. The fine automobile pictured here is a 1932 Cadillac V-8 sedan, featuring 'parlor doors' which mutually open from the center out. This beautiful car may not have been equipped with the fabled V-12 or the fabulous V-16, but it was powered by the engine that would outlive them both as standard equipment for the make that was destined to be the American luxury car, and would become the leading transportation for potentates the world over — no small feat, considering the competition presented by the Packard,

the Duesenberg, the Pierce-Arrow and a handful of other exquisitely-wrought luxury cars throughout the world.

The 'L-head' V-8 engine that powered some of the Cadillac line through the 1930s was of 342 cubic inches, with aluminum crankcase and iron cylinder heads. A final note on the V-16 was that Ernest Seaholm developed a new version of the engine in 1937. This advanced design had only half the number of moving parts as the original, and had 'L head' design. The V-16 was only produced until 1940, when both it and the V-12 were subsumed within the exigencies of war, never again to appear in a Cadillac automobile — often enough to appear in US Army tanks! The V-8 carried the day on the 'civilian front.'

Above: A 1934 Model 69 Graham sedan, with a supercharged straight eight. The supercharged Graham was the first production sedan to achieve 100 mph. The car is owned by Michael J Begley of Manhattan Beach, California. *Above opposite and below:* Though these coupes look similar, their historic importance is vastly different: the lower car is a 1934 Pontiac coupe, and the upper car is a 1935 Ford V-8 coupe, armed with the powerplant that made Ford Motor Company a legend—the flathead V-8

that would develop 110 horsepower. While the engine was introduced in 1932, and it took several years to get production and sales rolling smoothly — a typical Ford situation in the 1930s — the Fords of the 1930s were legends specifically because of the flathead V-8, an engine that was to be the Ford performance option until 1953. It was built to be improved over the years. Rugged and versatile, in the 1940s and 1950s it was the economy speed buff's 'hot rod' power plant.

From the ridiculous to the sublime. *At far left* is a 1934 Chrysler Airflow Imperial CV, which shows how much damage can be done by good intentions. The Imperial, the top-of-the-line Chrysler, did not deserve such treatment as the Airflow design offering. This is a perfect example of supposed efficiency really getting out of hand. The car was supposed to be a beautiful and elegant car, but given Airflow design, it misses the aesthetics mark by a wide margin — the front end design looks a great deal like the face of an alien on the cover of the cheap science fiction novels of the period.

Below, however, is the Airflow Chrysler with cosmetic 'beak' attached — the car actually looks sleek. It helped a lot to lower the car a touch, and the long limousine styling adds a lot to a body that, in the unmitigated Airflow designs looked 'high-hatted.' The only thing that's still wrong with the car is that terrible, utilitarian windshield.

These pages: An Art Deco Chrysler showroom of the 1930s. Note the various models shown here, and how the Airflow design did serve to round the corners off on the older, more classic, designs. One can tell by looking at this that the world was becoming just a bit less individual, as the Airflow cars also look as if they'd fit just fine into the scenario on a crowded freeway, while the older, more stately designs — quite handsome given their intended dignity — would look comic. One could say of the rounded corners of the Airflow that they are more anonymous than the adventurous curves of the older designs. This much-despised design was, ironically, widely copied in some of its aspects — note the rear views of several examples here: a few years later, this rear end would become almost generic! The Airflow design was destined to influence the basic look of cars in the late 1930s and 1940s, despite its public rejection. Tucked away into its startling exterior were some acceptable design ideas, after all.

Above and above right: This gleaming 1936 Dodge took three years effort to restore, and is based upon a completely original Dodge, including the paint and upholstery. The car is owned by Barbara Stubblefield of Mill Valley, California. Note the 'Airflow'-like blending of rear fender surfaces into the main carbody, and the relief provided by a standard, open front end on the car. The world of auto design was not yet ready to cope with the total 'Airflow' flat-fronted look just yet. *Below and below right:* This 1936 Ford four door V-8 sedan cost $400 to buy and took almost 19 years to restore. The owners of this gem are John and Patricia Davis, of San Lorenzo, California. The wondrous, mint-like paint used on this car was Ford's spring season color for 1936 — 'Armory Green.' Note the flowing lines of these cars, and the adjustable windshield on the Ford.

At left, left to right: A trio of 1936 Pontiacs at the stables — a six-cylinder two door sedan; an eight cylinder, four-door touring sedan; and a six cylinder coupe. By now, the flaring fenders of an earlier age were receding ever closer to the body, and headlights were seemingly trapped between the fender walls and the engine hood. Soon, headlight and fender would merge in a manner more dramatic than that so cleverly worked out on the 'coffin-nose' Cord. *At right:* A closeup of the 1936 Pontiac front end. *Below:* A 1936 six-cylinder roadster. As time went on, that long rear deck lid would become more likely to house a luggage compartment than a rumble seat, as the novelty of the automobile gradually wore off, and the motorcar began to settle down to more prosaic work than rides in the country. On this 1936 model, however, you could still seat two, with a modicum of comfort, in the rumble seat.

The sleek, sophisticated automobiles shown on these pages are both 1938 Buick Special Model 46-C convertibles. Buick was often enough second only to Chevrolet in sales at General Motors, and in 1934, new general Buick manager Harlow Curtice injected new vigor into an already worthy line of autos. The year 1938 brought Buick to the peak of American auto styling, as can been seen here. In addition to an impeccable appearance, improvements for the year included the new 'Dynaflash' straight eight with domed pistons and improved combustion chambers; all-coil front and rear spring suspension, semi-automatic transmission and an optional radio. The coach work seen on the two beautiful Buicks on these pages was done by European designers Letorneur et Marchand.

Packard was the sales leader of the luxury car makers, and the finest coachbuilders built on the Packard 12-cylinder chassis. Between the new 120-inch wheelbase model (the '120'), the Twin Six, the new six-cylinder and the straight eight, the Packard Company did well in the 1930s. Seen here are a rare and very beautiful 1940 Packard Darrin convertible cabriolet *(below opposite)*, designed by Howard Darrin. Larger models *(seen above and below)* carried the elegant Packard look to enviable extremes.

On these pages: This 1938 Packard touring car leaves no room to doubt that Packard had a standard of elegance and finesse that was far above many other auto manufacturers. The very look of this car gives one a sense of supple power and ease of movement — even so big a model as this gives the impression of a panther striding confidently through its domain. To own a classic Packard was — and is, especially now that they are long out of production — to know true automotive quality and prestige.

Pontiac was a good product for General Motors, and in 1940, its combination of an all-new eight cylinder and sophisticated 1940s styling made the erstwhile 'Chief of the Sixes' one of the overall American leaders in medium-priced car sales for that era. *At above opposite* is a brand-new 1939 Pontiac sedan, gleaming in the sunlight among the leaves somewhere in rural pre-war Michigan. *At left,* a couple of young wives admire the sleek good looks of a 1941 Pontiac convertible. The old fellow looking with interest at the 1940 Pontiac sedan *at top, above,* probably remembers the glory years of the first Pontiac straight-eight, in 1932. Note the 'moon' hubcaps and chrome 'beauty rings' on the wheels of these cars — a decorative touch that was quite popular in years gone by.

Ford's Lincoln Continental was a great design. The Continental was a product of the design studio which Henry Ford's son, Edsel, set up in 1933. Designer Eugene Gregory stylized the already very aerodynamic Lincoln Zephyr Convertible Coupe, taking a four-inch lateral slice out of the fenders and doors — this gave the new car a low-slung candor. The Continental's trademark exterior spare tire at the rear was then added. Each car was hand-constructed to exacting specifications. *Below and at right:* Two very beautiful early-1940s Lincoln Continentals.

These pages: A gleaming 1940 LaSalle shows very classy convertible styling and wide whitewalls that only looked good with the models of the 1930s and 1940s. This model year was the last for the car, which was essentially a lower priced Cadillac — and for that reason, the LaSalle line saw a steady decline in popularity in the late 1930s; for a few dollars more, you could own a *real* Cadillac. Still, there was a certain classiness about driving a LaSalle — if you couldn't afford a Cadillac, you could at least show that you wanted to afford one, and from a distance, the two lines were practically indistinguishable. The ultra-slim radiator shell shown here is the work of Harley Earl, General Motor's chief stylistic experimenter for years.

If you simply didn't care about technicalities such as prestige and class, you were in the market for an auto that had plenty of what Americans of the 1940s called *pizazz*—a certain low-priced liveliness that never failed to keep one's interest. Such an automobile is the 1941 Plymouth convertible shown on these pages. With a good little six cylinder under its hood, this car was perfect for the average person who wanted a little sportiness and light utility as well as dependability. Note the amber fog lamps and the famous Plymouth 'ship' ornament gracing the front of this car, Note also a fairly tasteful use of chrome here—obviously less restrained than on more expensive models, but also possessing a certain naive charm.

THE UNFORGETTABLE
1950s
(After the War)

The auto industry halted production in 1942 for the war effort, and retooled to supply the US war machine with tanks, trucks, jeeps, engines and munitions. After the war, the expanded facilities demanded increased sales; and America demanded cars as never before. The US had a new, mobile society — the war had opened America to the world at large, and to its own vast natural wealth. The American family vacation was thus born, and an ever-growing system of highways beckoned with a limitless variety of leisure time destinations. Beside the highways sprang up motels, hamburger stands and an entire highway culture that made sense only when viewed from an automobile. Chevrolet's sales pitch to 'See the USA in a Chevrolet' became an anthem.

World War II had also introduced the average American to vehicles that were amphibious, airplanes that flew near the speed of sound and weapons whose destructive fury seemed as potent as the Sun itself. Advances in rocketry and aerodynamics brought the age of space exploration suddenly near. The American public wanted cars that emanated a sense of stability and security, and yet invoked the dizzying excitement of the 'jet age' in which they suddenly found themselves. The 1947 Studebaker, with its 'greenhouse' windows mimicked the cockpit of a fighter plane, and the Buicks and Oldsmobiles offered rocket ship motifs and weightiness. Detroit and Dearborn fought competition from the 'Hot Rod,' the owner-customized car and the all-out European sports car. With performance packages, styling accents and the creation of such special models as the Chevrolet Corvette and the Ford Thunderbird, the American auto industry fought to expand its buying public. In particular, the Thunderbird awakened a dormant public desire for a sporty, yet reassuringly well-appointed car, and became as much an American bellwether as the merry, rumble-seated roadsters of days gone by. For most models of the second half of the 1940s and first half of the

1950s, if the car buyer knew that the car would not be outmoded too soon, he would buy it. Such designs as the Frazer of 1946 — like the Chrysler Airflow of the 1930s — influenced others, but did not sell. The classic, Raymond Loewy-designed Studebaker coupe of 1953 was lauded, and set a distinctive and unforgettable styling tone, but was likewise not a best-seller.

The pillarless look of the touring cars of old was resurrected in hardtop style on the 1949 Chrysler — and Buick — models, and soon the 'pillarless roof' was widespread. The early-to-mid-1950s Chevrolets and Fords had clean lines, and the 1955 Chevy stands out as a Chevrolet classic. Studebaker came out with an elegant, low-slung coupe in 1953, which was the design base for their famous high-performance 'Hawks,' and their handsome family sedans and coupes. The 1956 Chrysler offerings had daring but attractive styling. However, the *truly dominant* styling themes of the 1950s had their beginnings in General Motors' renditions of its higher-priced auto lines, which underscored an emotional approach to selling cars. Paul C Wilson, in his book, *Chrome Dreams*, puts it this way:

'Like an aborigine donning a horned and lurid ceremonial mask, the hen-pecked husband of suburbia happily climbed behind the wheel of his new 1950 Buick and set out to terrorize the populace. Few cars have had a more fearsome physiognomy: under a thick chromium lip its enormous mouth seems to stretch the metal skin above it in an effort to gape wider. Inside the mouth is a row of gleaming, carnivorous-looking fangs. Transformed from insignificance, the driver of such a car luxuriates in his disguise.'

Chrysler Corporation also soon took the plunge. Long, low and wide was the look, complete with GM-pioneered wraparound windshields. Ford Motor Company leaped into the garish fray in 1957, and in 1958, General Motors piled chrome onto its huge Oldsmobile and Buick models. Ford redesigned

its elegant Continental Mark II as the 1958 Continental Mark III, an outrageous inflation of the Mark II. Cadillac's Eldorado came as close to harmonizing tailfins, wraparound windshield and 'pillarless roof' as is humanly possible. The worst failure of the late 1950s was Ford's Edsel—with its 'horse collar' grille, it succumbed to the general ennui of an oversaturated public taste.

Sales for all makes in 1958 were terrible. Backlash resulted in an economy car boom in 1959–1960. The finned extravagance of the General Motors, Chrysler and Ford models made them classics of an age whose styling was based on fantasy and excess. Distinguished connoisseur of Americana Jacob Burke feels they were 'the very best cars, ever.'

Below opposite, this 1946 Mercury was of a type which would soon become popular as an American 'hot rod.' Somehow, the Mercury's familiar look and its V-8 engine combined to warm the heart of many a soldier returning from the war. Perhaps the fact that Ford and Chevrolet were the two most identifiably American automobile lines to be had, and that parts were readily available for autos manufactured by either of the two automotive giants, might have been primary inspirations motivating the phenomenon that autos from those two manufacturers were to become the standard vehicle for many a high-spirited ex-GI in search of speed, handling and sound parameters that simply weren't available straight from the showroom.

Seen *below* is a 1947 Studebaker Champion Regal Deluxe Coupe. Emphasis in post-war Studebakers was placed upon smooth handling, comfort and visibility—the latter of which gave rise to the extravagant amounts of glass used in these 'greenhouse' Studebakers, which caused a sensation when they first appeared. The company was to achieve a styling victory in 1953, with the Commander and Champion Starliner hardtop and starlight coupe—these two superbly designed automobiles were hailed as the styling achievements of the decade. Unfortunately, Studebaker's production line suffered delays, and the triumph did little to aid ailing Studebaker sales. Studebaker did, however, buy out the even more suffering Packard Company in 1954.

Another victim of the independent car company's struggles to compete with Ford, Chevrolet and Chrysler was the Kaiser-Frazer Company. The first model of the Kaiser-Frazer line was designed by Howard Darrin, the famous designer. This car won prestigious awards for its radically modern 'flat-sided' body, which was the precursor of most automobile designs since, and a good example of which is shown at bottom, below in the form of a late-1940s Frazer sedan. Though these cars were lauded for their looks, ride and comfort, the American public's attention had been—fatally for the independents—grabbed by the Big Three manufacturers. Kaiser-Frazer made fine cars, and early-1950s models had contoured seats front and rear and incredibly good visibility, but the company failed nonetheless.

These pages: This post-war Chrysler wood-paneled convertible was meant to be a classy car for the young family newly arrived in the suburbs—hence its model name, 'Town & Country.' At this time, however, Chryslers were not much more than inflated Plymouths, and their size gain would have made them look very boxy, but for such artful touches as the wood side paneling evident on this model. The Chrysler wasn't really distinguished at this point in its history for its powerplant—that would come shortly, in the form of the hemispherical combustion chamber overhead valve V-8 engine, and the wedge combustion chamber 318 cubic inch V-8 and its larger counterpart, the 395 cubic inch version. These were, however, years in the future.

For the time being, Chrysler built big family cars with lots of room for kids and more than enough steel to protect one's family in any conceivable accident.

Wood panelling was much in demand, the cold chill of war had only recently passed, and it was time for home, hearth and warm moods. Chrysler was betting on styling conservatism and comfort to carry its cars into the garages of its customers. And it was the era of the garage. Suburban living in the US was becoming a trend, and heavy, comfortable, dependable road cars such as the Chryslers shown on these pages were the very definition of security that the average American on the way up the social ladder sought. Note the extra trunk space and capacious roof rack on the 1945 models *shown at left and below*. The American family was ready for the 'family vacation' as it had never heretofore been experienced; never before had so many Americans been so mobile! And in such comfort! *At right* is a 1947 Chrysler carrying its passengers on a junket through the marvellous scenery of one of America's great mountain states, Montana.

When the 'Baby Boom' began to swell the population: *At right and below:* Looking over a 1947 Oldsmobile in the showroom. After World War II, Americans in unprecedented numbers formed families and had incredible numbers of children. Here we see two prospective family builders on the very brink of buying a General Motors car that was built for just such as they. The Oldsmobile 98 was a big, heavy car with a large straight-eight engine that developed 110 horsepower. Though these cars were not the fastest, they were loaded with low-end torque, and passing gear was a thrill, indeed. Also, Oldsmobile built cars with just as much solid comfort as the Chryslers, and with a touch more styling. These were fairly luxurious cars that would run for hundreds of thousands of miles, and were built to make the fellow with slightly higher than average income really feel that he was on the track of true success.

A car that almost looks more like a Cadillac than a Cadillac would ever dare to look! *These pages:* Three 1947 Lincoln Continentals. These were cars that were essentially designed to provide luxury and even more importantly than that, a luxurious look for their owners.

The 1948 Cadillac *(above)* introduced the first tailfin to American motoring. It was a controversial feature when it was introduced. It was the brain child of General Motors' vice president in charge of styling, who claimed that he got the idea from the famous World War II fighter plane, the Lockheed P-38 Lightning. *Below:* Believe it or not, a 1948 Tucker! It was one of many new ideas that blossomed in the wake of World War II — it was a new world, and Utopian designs, at first, seemed the order of the day.

These pages: A parade of Tuckers. The Tucker was scheduled to come out in 1948, but snared in legal complications, never made it to full production. It was quite advanced for its time, having not only a rear-mounted six cylinder engine with sextuple exhausts for greater efficiency, but also disc brakes and other such unusual features. The central headlight turned with the front wheels, giving the driver added road lighting. What appears here to be an engine hood here is actually a luggage compartment!

It was the era in which cars looked like people. The headlights of the 1951 DeSoto hardtop *at far left* combines with its hood ornament and toothy-looking grillwork to give one the impression of a rather pop-eyed face. The DeSoto was a slightly heavier version of the Plymouth, and as such, partook of the latter's general body lines. This was no accident on the part of Chrysler, it was a deliberate attempt to create a 'look,' which was exactly what Ford and General Motors were up to, for, in the post-war years, a new kind of war — among auto manufacturers — was beginning to brew. This was the war for the marketplace, and the more clearly identified your product was, the better. *Below:* A 1951 DeSoto convertible.

Ever conservative, Oldsmobile kept up its conservative ways. To own an Oldsmobile in the 1950s was to be recognized as a solid family man of conservative persuasion.

Oldsmobile partook of the major General Motors advance of 1949, the overhead valve V-8, and had considerable power for a family car. In fact, the heavy Oldsmobile and analogous cars such as the early 1950s Hudson were among the chief competitors on the American stock car racing tracks. The hot-rodder's practice (lifted from some of the famous sports cars of the 1920s and 1930s) of placing a huge engine in a miniscule chassis/body shell had not yet caught on with postwar American manufacturers. *On these pages:* A 1951 Oldsmobile Super 88 Deluxe sedan — a comfortable, reliable and handsome car for the not-quite rich.

In the late 1940s and early 1950s, the wide, low, substantial look was very much favored, especially in luxury cars such as the 1951 Lincoln *shown on these pages*. Note the recessed headlights and overall smoothness of body line. Ford was also much interested in improving the car's performance, and of course the Lincoln contained the top-of-the-line Ford V-8, a flathead as yet, but in a few short years, Ford V-8s would all be overhead valve engines. Due to its stylistic advantages over other Ford products, Lincolns such as the classy-looking car shown here became, as they were relegated to used car lots and such, the favorite models to be individualized by young men—in other words, they were, in the jargon, 'customized.' In short, they were some of the most popular 'hot rods' ever to be produced by unwitting manufacturers.

The Cadillac era: *Above opposite:* A fashionably blonde young lady sits in a 1952 Cadillac convertible. *Above:* A 1952 Cadillac four-door sedan. *At top, above:* A 1953 Cadillac Eldorado convertible owned by Ron Bledsoe of Walnut Creek, California.

In 1953, Studebaker produced a line of elegant coupes, designed by Raymond Loewy. These cars were widely acclaimed, but production problems slowed their marketing. *On these pages* is a mid-1950s Studebaker Commander, a fine example of the Studebaker Loewy coupe configuration. This low-centerline look was *the* Studebaker design, and was to be incorporated into the much sought-after Silver Hawk and Golden Hawk models (which added tailfins to this basic design) of the latter 1950s.

The low-slung coupe shown here presented as much a chance to feel sportscar-like closeness to the road as most American drivers would ever have in the 1950s, but what they wanted was something that looked more like a buffer against Cold War frigidity. Meanwhile, Studebaker's beautiful coupes — and not so sleek, but still nice-looking, family sedans — were bought by fewer and fewer customers.

Above: A 1955 Dodge Lancer. The Lancer design was but a harbinger of bigger tailfins to come! *Below:* This 1951 Dodge was a fairly popular model, and the price was right for the average income. *Above right:* A 1956 DeSoto, showing the basic lines that would define most Chrysler products in the late 1950s. *Below right:* A 1955 Plymouth. *Bottom right:* A 1955 Chrysler, before tailfins came to Chrysler.

Simple, forward-leading lines characterize these cars which were loved by many and hated by the competition. *Above left:* For the middle class market, this 1950 Ford convertible was the ideal 'fun' car for young people and budding families. *Below left:* The 1951 Ford Country Squire station wagon was a nearly archetypal family car of the early 1950s.

Below: This two-tone 1956 Fairlane Sunliner evidences the graceful simplicity of the better Ford designs; its 292 cubic-inch V-8 was a peppy little powerhouse, and was prized for its distinctive exhaust rumble. *Above:* This 1954 Mercury Monterey convertible evidences its status as the middle-range Ford product.

Left: The very nicely designed front end of a 1955 Chrysler Imperial, the top of the Chrysler range. Chrysler models had been equipped with the potent and legendary hemispherical combustion chamber ('hemi' for short) V-8 since 1952, which in later editions of Chryslers, boasted 300 horsepower straight from the showroom floor! The 1955 Imperial was a very prestigious-looking car, as is evidenced in the photos at *above and below*. Note the elegant restraint in the silhouette, the bumper-mounted exhaust ports and the innovative yet simple solution to taillight placement.

Above: A 1954 Buick Skylark, one of Buick's better style experiments in the 1950s. *Above right and below right:* Views of two more 1954 Skylarks, showing a different sort of Buick than most of us remember from the early 1950s. One hopes, of course, that the Skylark had something other between its V-8 and drive shaft than one of Buick's notoriously slushy 'Dyna-Flow' automatics. Those wire wheels are stock, and in 1954, Buick had a top-of-the-line 195 horsepower V-8. The sleek Skylark did not wear the fake fender-mounted exhaust ports that were a Buick trademark in the 1950s.

These pages: Advertising in the 1950s dictated clarity of image, and one of the techniques used here — to avoid blurring the car, but to get the feeling of motion, they focused in on the car parked in the middle of a road and had two people on a bike pedal by. Almost as clever as the Chevrolet Corvette which is featured here. This is a 1955 Corvette. The 1953–54 Corvette had a six-cylinder, but lacked a sophisticated sportscar undercarriage, and its automatic transmission seemed silly to sports car buffs; a manual transmission became standard in 1955. From the first, Corvettes had fiberglass body panels, and featured a two-seat cockpit. It was an appealing car. The first Corvette was exhibited in 1953, and sales were expected to be low. Were they to give a sale now, they'd sell many more than they did then, for this sporty-looking two-seater has become a classic. The Corvette was the first postwar all-American sportscar, and occupies a special place in the annals of American automobiles. Today's Corvette is of course a different beast altogether, and it makes one yearn for those (somewhat) more straightforward days of yore.

Chevrolet, of course, couldn't let the idea rest as a simple two-seat roadster. As we see in the photo *at left,* the company designed several hard top models and even a Corvette Nomad station wagon! Somehow, the slightly Bohemian look of the two-seat roadster version was more appealing, as one can judge from the photo above. As time went on, the 160 horsepower six cylinder was cast aside in favor of a V-8, as is witnessed by the dual exhausts issuing from the rear of the 1955 Corvette *shown below.* Among American cars, the early Corvette is a classic in its own right, and the sight of a 1954 or 1955 Corvette tooling down the boulevard causes a wave of nostalgia.

These pages: This 1955 Cadillac Eldorado Seville, with brougham styling, represented the apex of the Cadillac lineup. Its striking styling and smooth, clean lines caused many heads to turn — it looked like a Cadillac, but it was somehow too subtle to be anything but a limited edition car. This model eventually led to the front-wheel drive Eldorados of the 1960s, but in the 1950s, the model designation 'Eldorado' meant simply the very best and most stylish. As can be seen here, it was not a small car, but its sleek, low lines reduce the car's visual size dramatically, and give the impression of well-balanced, easy flowing power.

The Ford Thunderbird was not a sports car, but a car more in the tradition of the more dignified roadsters of old. It was small, intimate and had all the comforts of larger cars, plus considerable punch from its overhead valve V-8. It came in manual and automatic transmission versions, had dual exhausts and was generally thought of as *the* car to own if you were seeking to create a dashing image for yourself.

Above far left: A 1955 Thunderbird auto show winner. *Above:* A classic view of one of the well-proportioned early Thunderbirds, showing the seam line for the detachable hard top. *Below:* A 1955 Thunderbird, owned by Roy Kleffer of Santa Cruz, California, that has been on the show circuit in Northern and Southern California.

PSV·229

On these pages, we trace the beginning of the evolution of the Thunderbird—which resulted in the sleek family sedans which typify the Thunderbird lineup at the current time.

At above left, we have a typical 1955 Thunderbird, with its 292 cubic inch overhead valve V-8. Above: A 1957 Thunderbird. Note that the grillwork has enlarged, and the rear fenders flare out a bit. At below left, we have a 1958 Thunderbird, looking more like a jet aircraft, and less like the original, 1955, Thunderbird. Below, we have a view of the rear of a 1958 Thunderbird (see the photos on pages 134–135). These size and shape changes also brought bigger engines.

These pages: A 1956 Thunderbird in repose. Complete with whitewall tires and 'Continental kit' spare tire on the back bumper, this sporty little car is the apple of many an auto buff's eye. Available with numerous options, including electric windows and door locks, power steering, power brakes and a plethora of interior and exterior treatments, the 1955 Thunderbird was a brainchild of Ford designer *par excellence* Frank Hershey, and it was a design success that, even as it evolved, seemed to spark a popular magnetism. Almost more than any other American car, the 1955 Thunderbird invokes the spirit of an age that was somehow fresh and naive, and at the same time possessed an unusual sort of sophistication.

The Thunderbird, with its clean lines and rumbling dual exhausts seemed the distillation of everything that people liked about the early 1950s Fords, and its sporty size combined with the comforts enjoyed in much larger cars to grant this little two-seater a status and an exclusive appeal, even though it was manufactured in much larger numbers than was the limited-edition Corvette. In a peculiar way, the Thunderbird was just the enigma that American motorists had been waiting for: unexplainable, but as recognizable and as American as apple pie.

Cadillac continued to reign supreme in the luxury car field, and made improvements on the boxy designs of the late 1940s and early 1950s — the later cars partook of the low-slung lines which had been the mark of true luxury cars since the 1930s. Along with these design changes came increased tailfin size. The pronounced tailfins of the 1958 Eldorado Brougham *(above)* practically had trademark status. The years 1957–1960 were truly the era of the tailfin — seldom in motoring history has such a styling feature been so extolled *and* maligned!

The 1957 Cadillac convertible on the lower half of these pages evidences definitely increased tailfin size as compared with the 1956 Cadillac Sixty Special sedan *shown at right*. Note, too, how the body has been somewhat squared off, lengthened a bit and given a generally more low-slung look by

emphasizing the 'pancake' effect — all straight lines on upper surfaces (note this same effect on the Eldorado shown below) — this look was also popular on the larger late 1950s Chrysler Corporation models.

These were all cars that were made to give their owners the feeling that they were cruising the highways and city boulevards in their own living rooms, endowed with enough power to shoulder their way to the head of any line of traffic. The Cadillac of the 1950s was a refined car, but not a car for sissies; it was made to get its owners where they wanted to go, in the style to which they were accustomed and when they wanted to get there. It was no fluke that these were the cars chosen by heads of state throughout the world: Cadillac built luxury cars that gave the impression of easily-carried but extraordinary weight, and ample but unguessable power.

In contrast to those who sought conveyances of power, there was the light and frisky 1955 Chevy, which, with its clean but extremely pertinent lines was an instant design classic. With a new, upgraded Chevy six, this was a handsome, reliable car for the average person, a fine family car and just the thing to carry a carload of buddies on that fishing trip to the mountains. But the 1955 Chevy had another side, too. Chevy engineers Ed Cole and Harry Barr admired Chevy's old reliable 'stovebolt' six, surely — they just didn't think it had enough spunk. They went to work and came up with a revolutionary light V-8 design: the 265 Chevy, which weighed less than the 92/115 horsepower six, and cranked out 162 horsepower stock, and 180 horsepower with the Chevy option called 'Power-Pak,' which consisted of one four-barrel carburetor and dual exhausts. With the Ford V-8, the Chrysler hemi and the twin-carburetor Hudson Hornet, the 1955 Chevy became one of the classic 'factory hot rods' of the 1950s. The three photos *at right* show a 1955 Chevrolet Bel Air with a 'non-factory' hot rod treatment. Note the altered grillwork, magnesium alloy wheels and chrome tips on the exhaust — and attention-getting paint job! *Below* is the 'golden Bel Air,' the 50 millionth Chevrolet. The 1955 Chevrolet Bel Air is perhaps the classic American car of the 1950s. With few other cars is the indentification of an era with a car so strong, and reinforcing that is the fact that these little Chevys were nearly ubiquitous.

Above and above right: Two views of a 1956 Chevrolet Bel Air four door 'hot rod.' Its looks are 'classic Bel Air,' and an upgraded 265 V-8 probably nestles under its hood, although some of these earlier Chevys had their engines replaced by the 283 Cubic inch V-8 which came out in 1957, and was stock on such as the 1957 Bel Air Sport Coupe *shown below*. The legendary 283 was available in a fuel injected model that was rare, but was the first non-supercharged engine to claim (in full racing setup) a horsepower-to-cubic inch ratio of 1:1.

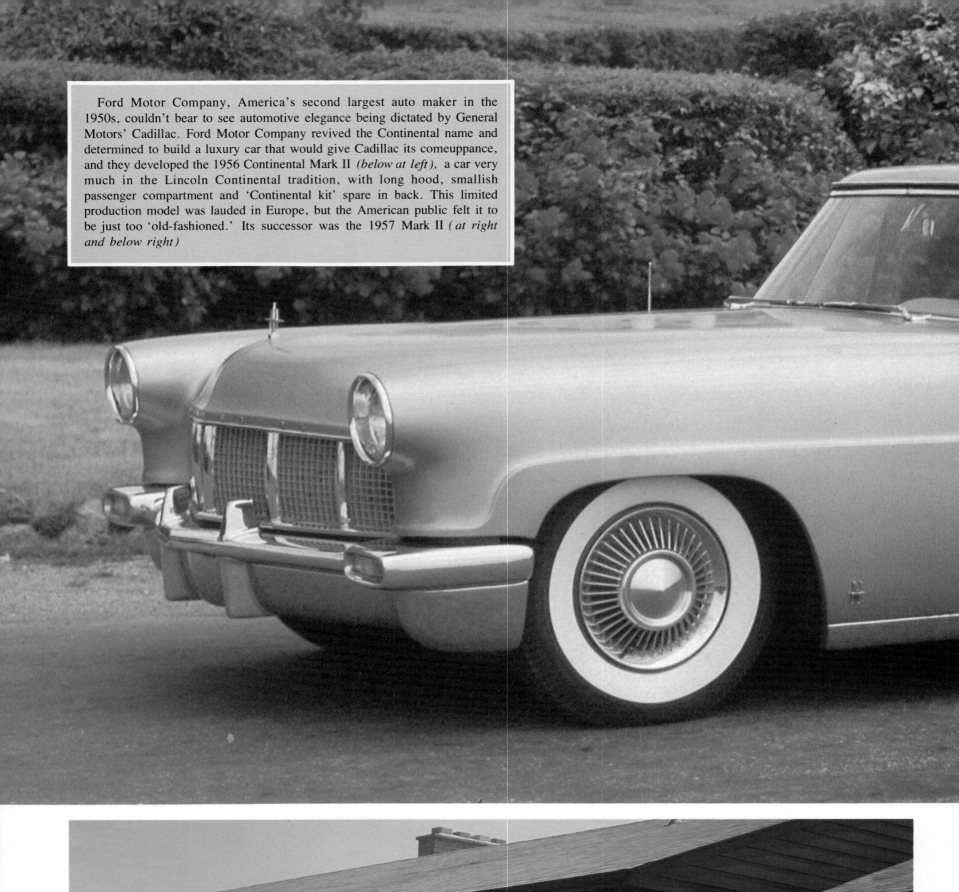

Ford Motor Company, America's second largest auto maker in the 1950s, couldn't bear to see automotive elegance being dictated by General Motors' Cadillac. Ford Motor Company revived the Continental name and determined to build a luxury car that would give Cadillac its comeuppance, and they developed the 1956 Continental Mark II *(below at left)*, a car very much in the Lincoln Continental tradition, with long hood, smallish passenger compartment and 'Continental kit' spare in back. This limited production model was lauded in Europe, but the American public felt it to be just too 'old-fashioned.' Its successor was the 1957 Mark II *(at right and below right)*

These pages: A 1956 Continental Mark II, the car that went largely ignored by the American public, but was felt by at least a few to be on par with such great classic American luxury cars as the Duesenberg and the Packard. It had a design based in simple elegance, a sense of lightness of line and a refined friendliness that was totally lacking in the incredible, huge 131-inch wheelbase 1958 Mark III, which is hardly in the same league, but did compete more successfully with the Cadillac. The Continental Mark II was not a small car, at 218 inches on a 126 inch wheelbase, but its design simply dealt with all that expanse in an interesting way!

In 1956, the Chevrolet Corvette had a more rakish look and a new 225 horsepower V-8 under its hood. A three-speed manual transmission became standard equipment and the Powerglide auto that had so plagued the Corvette's sports car image was now an option. 'America's sportscar' had other options, including a removable fiberglass hardtop and a power operated convertible top. In 1967, a specially-equipped Corvette took the Sports Car Club of America's Class B Production Championship, and dominated that class for eight years. The Corvette was still a limited production car, but with increasing engine size and more sophisticated mechanical equipment, it was to become one of America's most popular recreational cars. *Above:* A classic 1956 Corvette, in racing orange with white inserts. Note the distinctive 'hollow sides' look, which became an early Corvette trademark. *At far right:* A front view of a brother 1956 Corvette, showing the car's low road clearance and attractive front end.

It was indeed the time of the big car—as is witnessed by this view of a capacious 1955 Pontiac convertible *(above)* with a 180 horsepower V-8 and the patented 'Dual-Range Hydramatic' transmission. A few years later, the 1958 Bonneville convertible *(below)* was one of Pontiac's most popular cars, with its optional fuel-injected 348 cubic inch V-8, producing 315 horsepower. Interiors, too, were subject to some factory customizing, as the Leopard-skin treatment given this 1958 Pontiac Bonneville cockpit *(at left top)* attests.

Left: A 1959 Corvette, with some obvious 'hot rod' modifications, including altered suspension and magnesium alloy wheels. *Right:* A rear view of a 1958 Corvette. *Below:* Another 1958 Corvette, resplendent in a rural setting, with an attractive couple out for a jaunt in the country. Chevrolet's engines were getting bigger, and this year of course offered a fuel-injection setup and a good transmission.

Above and below, respectively: a 1958 Chevrolet Bel Air sedan and a 1958 Impala convertible. This was the year of Chevrolet's mighty 348 cubic inch V-8, and many customers rushed to the showroom to buy quantities of the Impala with the 348 under hood. Note the wide, flattened look of these 1958s, and compare that with their logical design conclusion, as seen in the 1959 Bel Air sedan at *above far right.* Also available as motive power for

Chevrolet standard models of 1958–1959 was the versatile 283 cubic inch V-8, with varying power options, and the reliable Chevy six. Note the rakish, sweeping lines on these cars, and their rather conservative use of 'lateral' fins, which conservatism Chevy had in common with Ford, and which, when the 1950s drew to a close, made it easy for both manufacturers to retool for the designs of the fin-abolishing 1960s.

The Edsel was meant to compete with the Oldsmobile and the Pontiac in the marketplace. Brought out very early in the model year 1958, the Edsel found its debut competing with other manufacturers' closeout sales, and its 'bug catching' grillwork was the subject of much derision, and its styling failed to create excitement among buyers.

Loaded with gadgets such as automatic transmission selector buttons located in its steering wheel hub and electric locks, doors and windows, the car's systems were fascinating, futuristic and complex. *Above left,* a 1958 Edsel Corsair and *below left,* a 1959 Corsair; *above and below,* 1958 Edsel Pacers.

Ford's Marketing Research Department contacted the renowned American poetess, Marianne Moore, in regard to the car's naming. Some of the names she came up with, in her tongue-in-cheek erudition, were 'The Resilient Bullet,' 'The Utopian Turtletop' and the 'Turcotingo' (for turquoise cotinga, the cotinga being a South American finch). In the end, Edsel adopted the name of Henry Ford's late son. The vertical grillwork harked back to the heyday of automotive styling, the 1920s and 1930s, which was also when Edsel Ford flourished—it was at his instigation that the styling department which conceived of the fabulous Lincoln Continental was formed. One popular criticism of the Edsel was that it didn't have a specific appeal—perhaps a more solid reason for the Edsel's failure as a model line was that it was fairly radical, a new proposition, and the industry was entering upon a sales slump. Its lines weren't really bad, but the radiator and very strange tail light styling took some getting used to. With a 361 cubic inch V-8 in the Edsel Pacer model, and with a whopping 410 cubic inch V-8 of 345 Horsepower in the Corsair and Citation models, these were cars that could at least go fast.

There are those who are devoted to the Edsel, however, and who cherish them even today as a prized possession. The Edsel has its own fan club, and owners give assurance that not all Edsels were prone to complex electronics systems maladies. Looking at a really well-kept Edsel such as the showroom condition 1958 Edsel Bermuda station wagon *shown on these pages,* one begins to doubt that the buying public was right in ignoring the Edsel. It does have a certain stylistic appeal, as can readily be seen by this two-tone wood-sided wagon, which is owned by Mr and Mrs Robert Castle Jr, of Acworth, Georgia.

On these pages are two views of one of the apocryphal cars of the 1950s, the 1957 Chrysler. This wide, long, huge-finned car exemplified everything that was excessive about the late 1950s. Its excesses did not stop on the surface, either. With a push-button Torqueflyte transmission attached to its monstrous 413 cubic inch hemispherical combustion chamber V-8, the huge car was the very epitome of that archetypal American slang designation, 'road hog.' This car had more torque and took up more room, caught more attention with its sweeping, radical silhouette than almost anything else on the highway. If you looked under hood at that gigantic engine, you would say that this car had a 'total effect' of vast excess!

The photos *on these pages* portray some of the most famous big-finned Cadillacs of all, the 1959 models. Note the massive grillwork, and the trademark twin 'bullet' taillights that suggest the exhaust flames of a rocket to the Moon! The airy brougham look was very popular among manufacturers of the late 1950s: note how the cantilever roof design works in dramatic counterpoint to the massive, thrusting front end and bold, brash fins. This was also the era of the all-power car, when even the trunk and hood latches could be made to obey the electrical impulse. Air bag shocks, increasingly sophisticated tires and a host of interior treatments made such as these late 1950s Cadillacs virtual travelling penthouses for their passengers. Engines with cubic capacities far in excess of their early-1950s forbears recalled cubic displacements of the early V-8s, V-12s, V-16s and straight eights. The beautifully preserved convertible shown in the views *above and above right* belongs to Ron Bledsoe of Walnut Creek, California.

SIMPLE LINES AND BIG HORSEPOWER

(The 1960s)

The really big news in the early 1960s was understated styling—and the mechanical specifications of a certain new Pontiac. Stylish and uncomplicated, Pontiac sedans in general seemed to fulfill exactly what was required of a car following the styling extravaganza of the 1950s. Eventually, the 'coke bottle' shape was adopted: the body was squeezed just slightly in the middle, giving it an elegant aerodynamic look.

European compacts had been selling heavily in the US, and of the compacts offered by US automakers, one was fated to give birth to a new genre of cars. The Pontiac Tempest—a compact answer to the Ford Falcon—gave birth, via a radical performance option package, to the Pontiac GTO, the first of the 1960s 'Muscle Cars'—compact- to medium-size sedans and coupes, factory-equipped with high-performance running gear. As Richard Nichols states in his *Classic American Cars*,

'The GTO quickly built up its own myth and became the subject of many pop songs . . . The GTO began to appear on TV programs like *My Three Sons* . . . it also set the trends for the way the rest of the musclecar (sic) breed was presented, marketed and hyped. The GTO was on the back of cornflake packets, was given away in competitions, was in stores everywhere as a model kit by Monogram, and . . . was the star of "Two-Lane Blacktop." '

The GTO was followed by the 327 and 409 cubic-inch Chevrolet Impala and Chevelle, and the 390 and 427 Ford Fairlane and Galaxy and Mercury Comet, and a steady succession of Chrysler Corporation Muscle Cars,

including the Plymouth Barracuda—eventually armed with the biggest 'muscle' of all, the 426 Hemispherical Combustion chamber engine.

The car that absolutely exemplified the Muscle Car motif was the Shelby GT Mustang, with modifications by the genius race car designer Carroll Shelby. The original Shelby Mustangs were formidable road cars, with their extremely high-performance engines, but Shelby eventually left the partnership, and mounting required Muscle Cars in general to sport 'de-tuned' engines. The 'Muscle Cars' soon went the route of substituting solid-looking bulk for raw racing ability, as critics of the high-powered machines gained public support. Before long, the 'Muscle Cars' (with an exception in the terrifically overpowered Hemi Barracuda) had to be content with looking and sounding fast, and little else.

In its non-'Muscle Car' versions, the cramped but very sporty-looking Mustang was bought by practically everybody, as it had an undeniable air of sprightliness that harked back through the decades to the 'gentleman's roadster.' Chevrolet copied the Mustang in their Camaro, which also copied the 289 cubic inch/306 horsepower Shelby Mustang with the Camaro Z-28 307 cubic inch high performance version.

The fastback roof, a styling fad in the late 1930s, made a comeback on the Buick Riviera, Corvette Stingray, Studebaker Avanti and was optional on the Mustang. The Riviera's styling was an up-scale version of the Mustang's roadster-like long hood and short rear deck, and competed with the Thunderbird. The Corvette's roof narrowed down to a point on its rear

deck, evoking the boattail roadsters of days gone by. The Avanti was a very striking and unique car—with its low-slung, supple and tastefully executed European contours—and still enjoys a dedicated following.

Hide-away headlights instilled some of the cachet of the Cord automobiles of 30 years before in such cars as the Corvette Stingray and the Oldsmobile Toronado—a front-wheel drive luxury car with battering-ram styling that took auto critics by storm. Pontiac had introduced its 'twin grille' look a few years earlier, and worked this motif into the distinctive Pontiac 'beak' of the mid-to-late 1960s. Fake radiators, attempting antique glamour, appeared on such cars as the extremely heavy 1968 Lincoln Continental Mark III, and Cadillac brought out its Eldorado of 1967, with gold-anodized wheel covers and trim. The full-size family sedan, now grown huge, became an ersatz luxury car, with soft upholstery, complex-looking instrument panel and plastic trim to mimic the fancy interior appointments of days gone by.

The once-again weary American public was on the brink of yet another stylistic crevasse—in the distance, a host of extremely plain sedans and compact cars thundered in from the horizon. Among them could be discerned the occasional, overdone late Muscle Car with its decals and fake hood scoops. This was a vision of what lay ahead in the decade of the 1970s, the classics of which are yet to be determined.

Suddenly it was 1963, and the Corvette Stingray *(these pages)* had arrived. It was a revolutionary design, bigger than most sports cars, and endowed with the sort of street car muscle that Detroit best knew how to provide—it was a drag racing road machine, the kind of peculiar hybrid that America produces from time to time to the astonishment of the world at large. Way back in 1959, General Motors stylist Bill Mitchell had crafted a Stingray body for a Corvette SS frame and entered the car, named the *Stingray*, in the President's Cup race at Marlboro Raceway in Maryland. The car placed fourth in that race, and after more racing, was placed on the auto show circuit in 1961. The production Stingray emerged shortly thereafter, with many of its progenitor's racing features incorporated—to the delight of anxious Stingray customers. The car featured fully independent suspension, fuel-injected engine and both convertible and coupe models *(as shown at right);* the only Stingray coupe to feature the now-classic split rear window being the 1963 model.

Pontiac entered the 1960s with a class act in the epochal 1964 GTO *(above and below).* In contrast to other manufacturers, who started to de-emphasize racing options in the late 1950s, Pontiac went straight for the high-performance youth market with an all-out offering of racing accessories. The GTO program got its start when a General Motors edict to Pontiac in 1963 said 'no more racing components—we're not in that business!' Pontiac sought a new angle to keep their sales going, and advertising man Jim Wangers and manager John De Lorean went to Pontiac engineer Peter Estes with a plan to put a big-block Pontiac 389 in the newly

evolved Tempest *(at left top),* normally a four-cylinder economy car, and the smallest in the Pontiac line.

The car was launched as the Tempest GTO, and was presented rather sneakily as merely a set of options—389 V-8 with three two-barrel carburetors and dual exhausts with a four-speed manual transmission. At first, it was presented to the Pontiac board with smaller engine specifications, but word leaked out to Pontiac dealers and orders began to flow in. The first year sales were the most for any first-year Pontiac model to that time, and the second year sales outdid that!

The Pontiac GTO was variously known throughout the 1960s as 'the Goat,' 'the Judge' and a host of other monikers, and above all, with its first-year rating of 348 bhp, the Pontiac GTO started the wild American fad of the Detroit 'Muscle Cars,' with such options as the GTO's factory-installed Hurst racing shifter.

Though sports car buffs hated Pontiac's use of the designation 'GTO' for a car that bore only slight resemblance to a classic sports car, the designation stuck, and prompted Pontiac to offer a ride package with the performance package. *On these pages,* various views of a 1966 GTO. Engines got bigger, transmission ratios improved and optional rear axles were available. Over the years, the GTO became more powerful, better styled, and more loaded with racing and handling options.

In 1963, the Buick Riviera appeared, and at the time it seemed a slightly more conservative fast back companion to the Corvette. Given more of a town car treatment and what had now become traditional Buick heaviness, the Buick still had considerable power and speed, with a large engine that was replaced (after the success of the GTO had convinced General Motors of the worth of the Muscle Car concept) by a standard 425 cubic inch version in 1965. This latter had a standard four-barrel carburetor, and was available with a second four barrel for a tremendous amount of high rpm power. Note the taut, clean lines of the 1963 Riviera *shown above*, and how these same lines have been improved upon in the 1965 Riviera *shown below*, by the subtle but effective step of filling in the false louvers in front of the car's rear wheel. Also, the headlights — which were located inboard of the front fender parking lights — became true 'hide-away' units in the 1965 Riviera.

These pages: The 1965 Mustang. Ford President Lee Iacocca knew that success lay in the production of a small, quick, easily-produced and low-priced car. Ford designers David Ash, Joe Oros and Gayle Halderman gave him what he wanted — a throwback to the roadsters of yesteryear, with long hood, a tiny cockpit and almost no room for luggage. In the days of the flathead V-8, Ford had reigned supreme, and now it was time for another Ford epoch! This was to be the epoch of the Mustang.

The Mustang was powered by a 170 cubic inch six, or an optional 260 V-8. In three basic styles including hardtop, convertible or fastback coupe, its first nine months of production saw an incredible 680,000 cars sold. Soon, the V-8 option had changed to include a 289 cubic V-8 capable of 271 horsepower, and this was the beginning of a performance progression which served to kick off Ford's commitment to its famous 'Total Performance' policy, and included an experimental Ford 'hemi.'

It was the success story of the decade, and General Motors and Chrysler had to play catch-up, but none could equal the tremendous cross-cultural appeal of the sporty, friendly and low-priced little Mustang. The car had an amazing range of options, including three or four speed floor shift manual transmission, handling package, power steering, air conditioning, bench or bucket seats, engine power options — basically, the customer could name his desire and get it with the Mustang. The hardtop coupe *shown on these pages* was the best selling version of the early Mustangs — at the turn of the decade into the 1970s, the clean, lean lines and much of the appeal of this little car would go the way of the Thunderbird. The year 1968 brought the Mustang big engines — a 335 horsepower 390 V-8, and a 390 horsepower 427 cubic inch V-8 — and those that really had high performance were

usually those that Carroll Shelby, father of the aptly named Shelby Cobra sportscars, had stamped with his signature logo, a coiled cobra. So, the Mustang was a car that your little sister could drive, and it was also a car that could outperform any other car on the road. With so much variety to choose from, it's no wonder that Ford's Mustang had an entire auto sales bracket all to itself from 1965 – 1967, and it sold phenomenally.

Mustangs set records everywhere. *Above and at right:* Shelby GT Mustangs like these were the ones to watch out for in the late 1960s. Shelby's phenomenal 'Cobra treatment' affected several versions of the Mustang, and meant uncompromising performance. A maximum perform-ance 289 cubic inch engine powered the GT 350 (which had 306 horsepower) and a maximum-performance 428 powered the GT 500. Shelby's Cobra Mustang line was dropped by Ford in 1967, but Shelby stayed with the GT convertibles. While management at Ford eventually took steps to de-tune some of these cars, they were still impressive. *Below:* A standard 1968 Mustang fastback.

The 1962 Studebaker Gran Turismo Hawk *(above left)* borrowed heavy rear roof pillars from the Thunderbird, and added a fake front grille, and wound up as a car that was sleeker than the Thunderbird, by far. One of Studebaker's heaviest liabilities was its plant location in South Bend, Indiana—away from the well-developed materials and parts supply lines of Michigan's great automaking centers, Dearborn and Detroit.

The favorite on many auto buffs' lists was also the last—the legendary 1963 Avanti *(above and below)*, which set several speed records. Its sleek, European-inspired lines were the product of the design genius of Raymond Loewy. Inside, aircraft-style instrument panels were located on the dash and above the windshield as well, which was well suited for a car that included a supercharger in its optional equipment, and was known to hit 170 mph at the racetrack. Thanks to the efforts of two South Bend Studebaker dealers, Avanti production continued past the demise of its parent company in 1965. Asked what it is like to drive his car, an Avanti owner in Williamsport, Pennsylvania, replied 'It's absolutely wonderful.'

Above far left: The 1965 Plymouth Barracuda. Initially, the Barracuda featured either of two six cylinders or a 180 horsepower 273 cubic inch V-8. Its second year saw the Formula S package, which upped the 273 to 235 horsepower and gave the car a pretty good handling package. Plymouth soon reintroduced that old Chrysler Corporation staple, the hemispherical combustion chamber V-8, only this time in a 426 cubic inch version that delivered 425 horsepower! *At top and above:* A 1967 Barracuda.

In 1967, Chevrolet brought out their answer to the Mustang and the Barracuda. This car was known as the Camaro, and true to form, this model had an incredibly long list of options, so that the buyer could essentially tailor the car to his fancy. Officially, the basic engines available were a 140/155 bhp straight six and two V-8s, in 327 and 350 cubic inch versions. There was, however, a third option that was rather quietly introduced — this was the brand-new high-performance small block V-8, which seemed tailor made (and it was) for the Trans-Am racing series, despite Chevrolet's then-recent anti-racing avowals. This engine, just over 300 cubic inches, formed the heart of the famed Z-28 racing package, which would represent the top of Camaro form until many years later. The original Z-28 was of no use to anyone but an all-out racer, although in later years, the designation was used to sell more ornate Camaros with streetable, huge V-8s. With everything from a six to a high performance V-8, the Camaro truly was Chevrolet's answer to the Mustang. *At left:* A 1967 Camaro SS convertible. *Below:* A 1969 Camaro coupe.

General Motors management talked Pontiac into making a Camaro lookalike, and the Firebird was born. At this stage, the Firebird's top-of-the-line engine was a 335 horsepower V-8, later replaced by a 360 horsepower V-8 (actually, following GM's dictum of no more than one horsepower per 10 pounds of body weight, Pontiac fitted a soft metal tab to the carburetor of their 360 horsepower engine to create the 335 horsepower version — this tab was often removed by those who knew about it). In 1968, there was a 400 HO (High Output) Camaro, and numerous performance kits were brought out to improve the Firebird's performance, and in 1969, the 400 HO Firebird became the 400 Ram Air HO 11, which put out 340 horsepower. *Above and below:* 1968 Firebirds; *above right:* A 1969 model.

At left and above left: Views of a 1968 Pontiac GTO. *At top, above:* A 1969 GTO convertible, Pontiac's tried and true 'Muscle Car,' showing the plastic nose piece that was installed that year on both the GTO and Firebird models. When Ferrari took exception to the use of *Grand Turismo Olmogato* — GTO — Pontiac arranged a test between the two cars. En route, the Pontiac blew a piston, and a huge Pontiac Catalina stood in for it, out-drag racing the Ferrari, but understandably much less agile! The GTO's three two barrel carburetors operated in the following way: for cruising, only the central two-barrel was in operation. At very high rpms, or when the accelerator was trod suddenly, the additional carburetors opened up.

These pages: A 1968 Corvette, with the 'Mako Shark' show-car styling that replaced the 'Stingray' look that year (although the cars were still officially Corvette Stingrays). It was the Corvette's 15th anniversary, and a lot of changes had been made. The car was larger, heavier and had dramatically larger engines, including the Chevrolet 396 semi-hemi head engine, which was informally known as the 'porcupine' or 'rat' Chevy. Like most other special Detroit models, the Corvette came with a long list of options, but in its case, the options were predominately engineering parts—gear ratios, suspension packages and engine parts. This served to keep the Corvette on track as a competitive sports car, although it was larger than many. Corvettes also saw plenty of action at the drag strip and in road racing. All in all, the Corvette of the 1960s continued to build a legend.

INDEX

Ash, John 174
Auburn 42 – 43, 59
    Cabriolet 46 – 47
    851 Boattail Speedster 46 – 47
Austin, American 69
    Bantam 69
Barr, Harry 142
Begley, Michael J 72
Bentley 32
Bledsoe, Ron 121, 164
Breer, Carl 59
Bridges, Jeff 110
Buick Skylark 126 – 127
    Special 82 – 83
Cadillac 1, 12 – 13, 15, 35, 56 – 57, 120 – 121,
    164 – 165
    Eldorado 121
    Eldorado Brougham 140
    Eldorado Seville 132 – 133
    Sixty Special 140 – 141
    V-8 Sedan 70 – 71
Castle, Mr and Mrs Robert J 161
Chevrolet, Louis 17
Chevrolet 17
    Bel Air 122, 142 – 143, 144 – 145, 156, 192
    Camaro 184 – 185
    Corvette 128 – 129, 131, 150 – 151, 154 – 155,
    190 – 191
    Impala 156
    Nomad station wagon 130
    Stingray 166 – 167
Chrysler, Walter P 61
Chrysler 32, 162 – 163
    Airflow Imperial CV 74 – 77, 98 – 101, 123
    1926 Imperial 80 Coupe 32, 36
    Imperial 124 – 125, 176
    Le Baron CH 60 – 61
    1929 Roadster 36 – 37, 97
Cole, Ed 142
Cord, Erret 43, 49, 51
Cord 812 Berline 50 – 51
    812 Phaeton 52 – 53
Curtice, Harlow 83
Darrin, Howard 85
Davis, John and Patricia 78
Daytona Beach 11
De Lorean, John 169, 186
De Soto 61, 112 – 113, 123
Dodge, John and Horace 15
Dodge Victory Six 33, 61
    Lancer 78 – 79, 122
Duesenberg SJ Roadster 1, 48 – 49, 53, 59, 70, 149
Durant, WC 17
Estes, Peter 169
Ferrari 189
Ford, Edsel 35, 161
Ford, Henry 15, 22, 27, 35, 161
Ford 118, 134 – 139
    Model A 13, 14 – 15, 20, 26 – 27
    1927 Model A 28 – 29
    Model T 18 – 19, 20 – 23
    V-8 73, 78 – 79
    Country Squire 118

Fairlane Sunliner 119
Mustang 53, 149, 174 – 177, 185 – 186
Shelby Cobra 176
Shelby GT 178 – 179
Thunderbird 4 – 5
Fortes, Manuel and Adele 69
Foster, William H 11
1928 Franklin 32
Frazer Sedan 97
Fuller, R Buckminster 110
    Dymaxion cars 110
Gable, Clark 49
General Motors 25, 83, 89, 102, 147, 167, 176
1934 Graham Sedan Model 69 72
Gregory, Eugene 90
Halderman, Gayle 174
Hanson, Jack L 47
Hershey, Frank 139
Iacocca, Lee 174
Indianapolis Track 51
Jenkins, AB 63
Kleffer, Roy 135
La Salle 92 – 93
Leland, Henry Martyn 13
Lincoln Continental 22, 34 – 35, 90 – 91, 114 – 115
    Continental Mark II 146 – 149
    Cougar 186
    Mercury 96
    Monterey 119
    1931 Roadster 54 – 55, 104 – 105
Marlboro Raceway (Maryland) 167
Miller, Harry 51
Mitchell, Bill 167
Oakland Six 24
Oldfield, Barney 15
Olds, Ransom E 11
Oldsmobile Limited 10 – 11
    Standard Runabout 11 (advertisement)
    Starfire 6 – 7
    Super 88 Deluxe Sedan 116 – 117
    Toronado 102 – 103, 180 – 181
Oros, Joe 174
Overland, Willys 69
Packard 2 – 3, 35, 38 – 39, 149
    Darrin convertible cabriolet 84 – 85, 97
    1933 V-12 Touring car 40 – 41, 59, 70, 86 – 87
Pierce-Arrow coupe 63 – 65
    roadster 66 – 67, 70
Plymouth Barracuda 61, 94 – 95, 113, 123, 182 – 183
Pontiac 25, 68 – 69, 72 – 73, 80 – 81, 88 – 89
    Bonneville 152 – 153
    Firebird 186 – 187
    GTO 168 – 171, 186
    Le Mans 30
    Riviera 172 – 173
    389 168
Rolls Royce 35
Seaholm, Ernest 57, 71
Shannon, Josephine M 69
Shelby, Carroll 176
Silver Arrow 63
Stubblefield, Barbara 78
Studebaker 97, 105
Stutz Bearcat 30
    Blackhawk 30
    Roadster 30 – 31, 32

Tucker 106 – 111
Van Ranst, Carl 51
Wangers, Jim 169
Whippet Model 96 Coupe 68
Winton, Alexander 11

Picture Credits

Below: The classic 1955 Chevrolet Bel Air four-door sedan.

1915 Buick

1916 Oldsmobile

1917 Oakland

1921 Case

1922 Mercer

1923 Stearns

1927 Jordan

1928 Ford Model "A"

1929 Plymouth

1933 Dodge

1934 Chrysler Airflow

1935 Cadillac

1939 Packard

1940 Mercury

1941 Plymouth

1947 Kaiser

1948 Dodge

1949 Ford

1953 Mercury

1954 Chrysler

1955 Chevrolet Bel Air

1959 AMC Rambler

1960 Plymouth Valiant

1961 Willys